This book is to be returned on or before
the l...

Withdrawn

Fireplace

Design and Construction

Charlotte Baden-Powell AADip RIBA

George Godwin
London and New York

George Godwin
an imprint of:
Longman Group Limited
Longman House, Burnt Mill, Harlow
Essex CM20 2JE, England
Associated companies throughout the world

*Published in the United States of America
by Longman Inc., New York*

First published 1984

British Library Cataloguing in Publication Data
Baden-Powell, Charlotte
   Fireplace design and construction.
   1. Fireplaces – Great Britain – Design and construction
   I. Title
   697'.1   TH7425

    ISBN 0–7114–5619–4

Library of Congress Cataloging in Publication Data
Baden-Powell, Charlotte, 1936–
Fireplace design and construction.

   Bibliography: p.
   Includes index.
   1. Fireplaces – Design and construction.   I. Title.
TH7425.B28 1984   697'.1   83–5449
ISBN 0–7114–5619–4

Set in 10/12pt Linotron 202 Garamond 3 Roman
Printed in Britain by Pitman Press (Bath)

To talk of architecture is but a joke
Till you can build a chimney that won't smoke

CONTENTS

Contents

*All line drawings except for Figs 1.20 and 9.14
were drawn by the author.*

ACKNOWLEDGEMENTS

We are indebted to the following for permission to reproduce copyright material:

Frilandsmuseet for frontispiece (a); Alberto Ponis for frontispiece (b); John Webb for our Fig. 1.8; *Country Life* for our Figs 1.9, 1.10, 1.11, 1.12, 1.16, 1.17 and 10.14; T. & R. Annan and Sons Ltd for our Fig. 1.18; Paul Mayen and the Western Pennsylvania Conservancy for our Fig. 1.19; Controller of Her Majesty's Stationery Office for our Fig. 2.1; Solid Fuel Advisory Service for our Fig. 3.2; Baxi Heating for our Figs 4.18 and 9.4; Jeremy Dixon for our Fig. 6.3; Selkirk Metalbestos for our Fig. 7.9; Glynwed Appliances Ltd for our Fig. 9.2; A. Bell & Co. Ltd for our Figs 9.6 and 9.28; T. I. Parkray for our Fig. 9.7 and 9.17; Jetmaster Fires Ltd for our Fig 9.9; Keddy Home Improvements Ltd for our Fig. 9.11; Norcem (UK) Ltd for our Figs 9.12 and 9.20; Real Flame for our Figs 9.13 and 9.14; Smith and Wellstood Ltd for our Figs 9.16, 9.22 and 9.30; Hunter and Son (Mells) Ltd for our Fig. 9.19; Godin SA for our Figs 9.21 and 9.25; Philip Spencer Stoves Ltd for our Fig. 9.23; H. Krog Iversen and Co. for our Figs 9.24 and 10.16; Quebb Stoves for our Fig. 9.26; Trianco Redfyre Ltd for our Figs 9.27 and 9.29; Victoria Stone Ltd for our Fig. 10.1; Minsterstone for our Fig. 10.3; Acquisitions Fireplaces Ltd for our Fig. 10.4; Patrick Fireplaces for our Fig. 10.5; Roger Pearson for our Fig. 10.6; and Galleon Claygate Ltd for our Fig. 10.10.

The author would personally like to thank L. J. Jacobsen, formerly of the National Coal Board, for his invaluable help and advice and the many manufacturers and suppliers who provided so much information and photographic material.

Frontispiece (a) The focus of the home, a central fireplace in a Danish farmhouse of 1688 (*Frilandsmuseet*).

INTRODUCTION

From earliest times, the fire has been the focus around which man gathered to keep warm and to cook his food. Indeed the word 'focus' is Latin for fireplace.

The open fire has been particularly loved by the British, more so than by the Europeans who developed the closed stove, possibly because of their need to have a more efficient way of heating their house, especially through long months of below-freezing temperatures, whereas, in Britain, the vagaries of the weather and the relatively mild winters have made the open fire a feasible form of heating and one which cannot be surpassed for sheer enjoyment and fascination.

Since central heating became more widespread, many fireplaces have been blocked up and often new houses are not built with chimneys but, now that the running costs of central heating continue to rise, people are constantly looking for ways of heating their houses more economically. Many are opening up their fireplaces, and new houses, or houses without chimneys, are being fitted with chimneys once more.

Modern methods of firelighting and ash collection, more efficient grates and insulated flues have largely eradicated some of the less-attractive aspects of the traditional open fire, namely the difficulty of lighting, poor draught and smoky rooms.

So with this reawakened interest in the open fireplace, this book aims to provide complete information to both the layman and the professional.

It is hoped that architects, designers and builders will find this book as useful for installing or rehabilitating fireplaces as people who wish to install or improve a fireplace themselves.

To put the fireplace in perspective there is a short historical section, which is followed by planning and design guides including explanations of the UK Building Regulations. There is a section about fuel and fuel storage and information about fireplace accessories. Finally there are indices giving advice sources, manufacturers' addresses and a bibliography.

Frontispiece (b) A house designed by Alberto Ponis in 1974 with several intercommunicating levels; the fireplace is still, however, the visual focal point, as in the much earlier Danish fireplace in frontispiece (a) (*Alberto Ponis*).

Chapter 1

HISTORY OF THE FIREPLACE

From earliest times the open fire was generally placed in the centre of the dwelling. The Laplander and the American Indian still make their fires in the centre of their tents, allowing smoke to escape through the top. Some of these tents have quite sophisticated systems of flaps, allowing different amounts and direction of draught to enter at low level and adjustable funnels at the top allowing the flue direction to be altered according to the velocity and direction of the wind.

The earliest British hearths were generally made of clay placed in the centre of circular wooden or stone huts.

When the Romans came, they heated their villas with hypocausts. These were spaces under floors heated by outside furnaces (Fig. 1.1). Alternatively they used charcoal braziers which could be moved from room to room.

Curiously, the Saxons failed to imitate the Romans' innovatory way of heating their houses, possibly because most of their Saxon houses were built in wood and plaster, rather than stone. The fire was made in the centre of the main body of the house and the smoke drifted out of unglazed windows or a hole in the roof (Fig. 1.2).

The fear of the houses catching fire was ever present and in 1068 William the Conqueror introduced a law requiring a curfew (or *Couvre-feu*) which was a metal cover to be put over the fires to extinguish them at night (Fig. 1.3). A bell was rung at 7 p.m. for this purpose. The law was also intended to discourage 'nocturnal assemblies' where revolutionaries might gather to plot against the new king. From this came our present use of the word curfew, ascribed to the act of keeping people in their houses, rather than the putting out of fires.

As the design of houses developed in the thirteenth century, windows were fitted with glass and shutters, making it impossible for smoke to clear the rooms, so small turrets were built into the roof ridge directly over the hearth. These turrets were fitted with louvres (from the French *l'ouvert*) to prevent the rain coming in but to allow the smoke to get out (Fig. 1.4). Smaller rooms were sometimes heated with charcoal braziers. As charcoal burns with little smoke, the need for an extract was less necessary.

3

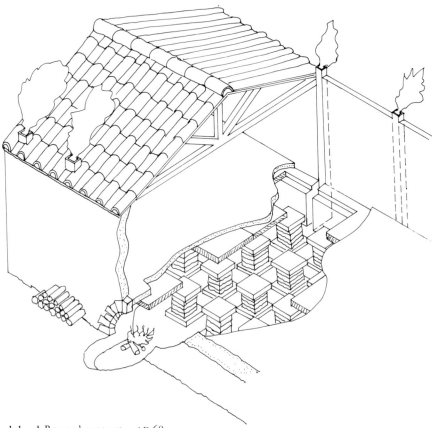

1.1   A Roman hypocaust *c.* AD 60.

Soon after the Norman conquest the fireplace moved to the wall, although the central fireplace continued right through to the end of the fourteenth century (Fig. 1.5). Moving the fireplace to the wall probably came about because of the impossibility of having a central fireplace without a chimney in a two-storey building. These early wall fireplaces were extracted by diagonal funnels carrying the smoke up through the thick walls to an opening higher up in the wall (Fig. 1.6). Where fireplaces were placed in circular walls within keeps, it was easier to build a straight lintel over the fireplace opening, rather than follow the curve of the wall, hence a hood had to be formed to guide the smoke back up to the opening in the wall (Fig. 1.7).

A few of these early fireplaces had tall cylindrical shafts, which seem to be the earliest form of chimney as we know it. The word chimney comes from the French *Cheminée* which referred to the hearth and flue, not just to the flue as in current usage.

The fireplace in the wall, with hoods made of various materials, first stone and sometimes wood and plaster, continued until towards the end of the fourteenth century when it was discovered that it was possible to recess the fireplace fully within the thickness of the wall with an arch or lintel flush with the wall, getting rid of the hood

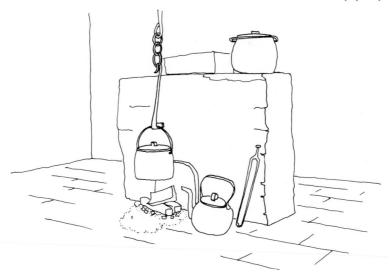

1.2   A central hearth with stone reredos in the Orkneys, still in use at the end of the nineteenth century.

1.3   A curfew or *Couvre-feu* made of repoussé brass, late seventeenth century, Brighton Museum.

altogether. The hearths were raised slightly and iron dogs or 'andirons' (see p. 125) supported timber logs, raising them slightly so that air could get underneath and improve combustion. In the late fifteenth century chimneys became taller and, as walls became thinner, so it became necessary to protect the chimney on the outside of the wall.

In the sixteenth century the brick chimney was developed. Chimney stacks containing several shafts served an increasing number of fireplaces.

In medieval times the fireplace needed to be large enough to roast whole beasts. The carcasses were supported on spit jacks which were turned by small boys. Later developments included ingenious devices such as a fan, placed in the mouth of the chimney and activated by the draught from the fire, which turned a rod connected to the spit. In Pembrokeshire, small dogs were trained to turn a treadwheel placed high in the wall of

1.4   Abingdon Abbey *c.* 1260
       Gabled chimney stack with lancet-shaped openings. At the left of the stack, a flue outlet
       made of vertical stones supported on corbels from a fireplace, used to heat the wine, in the
       crypt.

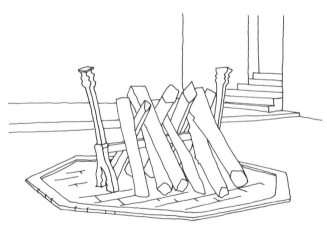

1.5   Penshurst Place 1340
       Central hearth in the great hall, with coupled andirons.

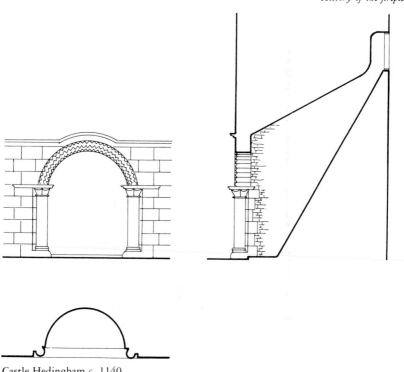

1.6   Castle Hedingham *c.* 1140
A diagonal flue – from a drawing by L. A. Shuffrey in The English Fireplace and its Accessories.

the fireplace. This wheel was connected to the spit by a chain passing over a block (Fig. 1.8)

The Normans introduced more elaborate menus to England, so cooking became more important. Large numbers of family and staff had to be fed. Some halls had more than one fireplace so that roasts could be done in one, boiling in another and baking in separate ovens. At first ovens were spaces made under brick or stone hearths, but they were soon moved into the side walls alongside the open fire. These ovens, which can still be seen in old cottages today, were used for baking bread. A fire was made inside with faggots and the smoke escaped through the door up the chimney over the open fire. When the oven was hot enough, the ashes were raked out and the bread baked in the residual heat.

As house plans became more sophisticated, so the cooking was banished to kitchens, sometimes in separate buildings. This meant that the fireplace was used primarily for house heating only and as a focus for social life, and it became a status symbol in which many arts and crafts were skilfully displayed. In Elizabethan times, Flemish and German craftsmen were introduced to decorate the fireplace. The stone arch or oak lintel over the fireplace was finely carved, the space over the lintel was at first hung with fine tapestries and later in Jacobean times covered with elaborate plasterwork often incorporating the coat of arms or heraldic devices of the family (Fig. 1.9).

1.7   Aigues-Mortes, France *c.* 1250
   A stone hood in the lower hall or the tower of Constance, elegantly integrated with the
   corbel of the vaulted roof.

Fireplaces, where stone was not available, were lined with bricks or tiles. In the early sixteenth century iron foundries were developed in the Weald of Sussex which produced a great range of fireplace accessories including the iron fireback which was often ornamented with great individuality.

At the beginning of the seventeenth century wood became scarce and sea-borne coal came into domestic use, so the fire basket was devised to burn it and shovels and tongs were introduced to handle it.

1.8 A kitchen fireplace in Newcastle, South Wales, Aquatint by Thomas Rowlandson in 1797 showing a dog employed as a turnspit (*John Webb*).

After the great fire in London in 1666, houses were rebuilt in stone or brick and most rooms were provided with smaller fireplaces for burning coal, which by now had become the staple fuel in towns.

The fireplace continued to be a vehicle for rich decoration. Inigo Jones imported marble fireplace surrounds carved in Italy. Christopher Wren introduced the mirror and shelves for displaying china, to the overmantel. Sometimes these overmantels were decorated with elaborate wooden festoons as carved by Grinling Gibbons.

With the acceptance of neo-classical design, by the beginning of the eighteenth century, many domestic fireplaces had surrounds with flat pilasters and consoles supporting entablatures carved in wood and marble. Sometimes even caryatids supported these shelf entablatures (Fig. 1.10).

During the eighteenth century, pattern books were published for internal decorations, many including very flamboyant designs for fireplaces.

In 1742 and 1773 the Adam Brothers published *Works in Architecture* introducing purer classical designs. Their designs showed a refinement of detail with the use of white marble with yellow and green inlays. Overmantels included large mirrors in light gilt frames, figures or medallions. Other designs showed stucco ornamentation blending into the decoration of the whole room. Their work had widespread influence and many of their designs were copied. During the eighteenth century great progress was made in the design and manufacture of fire grates, which were either the basket type or the hob grate (Figs. 1.11, 1.12 and 1.13).

However, the problem of smoking fireplaces continued and in the mid-eighteenth century two great men put their minds to this problem.

Shortage of wood fuel on the East coast of America caused Benjamin Franklin to look

1.9 Loseley House, Surrey
Late Elizabethan chimney piece carved from a single block of clunch incorporating caryatids, heraldry and classical features with great exuberance (*By kind permission of Country Life*).

more closely at the open fire. He reasoned that the traditional fireplace allowed too much hot air to escape up the chimney, instead of warming the room. To counteract this he developed one of the first dampers, a sliding door to restrict the flow of hot air between the fire and the flue. He also recognised that the closed stoves introduced by

1.10   Mawley Hall, Shropshire *c.* 1730
        The overmantel is decorated with a trophy of Roman arms and armour and the frieze
        with astronomical instruments and flowers. This chimney piece is beautifully integrated
        with the architecture of the room as a whole (*By kind permission of Country Life*).

German immigrants were more efficient in their use of fuel, but felt they were unhealthy
as they created a stuffy atmosphere, not allowing natural ventilation as did the open fire.

He observed that in wood fires, flames burn in long tongues so that most of the flame
is lost up the chimney. He also noted that wood burns in three stages. First, moisture is
evaporated before wood will ignite, secondly the volatile oils such as turpentine in pine
logs must vaporize and burn and will rise quickly, producing a tongue of flame. Often
these oils and water vapour will escape the firebed before they are completely burnt,
producing smoke or creosote. Thirdly, the final stage is the combustion of the charcoal,
by now virtually pure carbon, which burns with little smoke or visible flame but gives
off a lot of heat. So, to improve the efficiency of burning wood, he invented a freestanding fireplace which evolved into the 'Franklin Stove'.

1.11   Combe, Devon *c.* 1760
A carved pine rococo chimney piece with a mirror, candle brackets, bird's nest, Chinese
ho-ho birds and a little mouse viewing itself in the mirror (*By kind permission of Country
Life*).

1.12 Arbury Hall, Warwickshire 1762
A neo-Gothic room with the fireplace based on the tomb of Aymer de Valence in
Westminster Abbey of 1384 (*By kind permission of Country Life*).

1.13 A typical late eighteenth-century hob grate.

This stove, in effect, was an open fire within a metal box set in front of a bricked-up
fireplace. The stove attempted to assure complete combustion by containing the flame
and smoke within the firebox as long as possible. A baffle was placed halfway back in
the box, either as a steel plate or a brick wall. The products of combustion were taken
down and out into the chimney, making the flame and smoke pass all around the
firebox, allowing more time for the wood to burn more thoroughly. The cast-iron
casing gave off heat into the room and, in some versions, air was drawn up from the

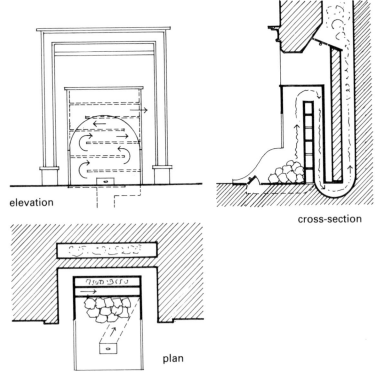

elevation

cross-section

plan

1.14   Benjamin Franklin's 'Pennsylvania Fireplace' 1742
The firebox had a baffle of 'caliducts' in which air circulated, drawn in from an
underfloor duct. The smoke from the fire was forced down and under a brick wall before
rising into the flue.

cellar below to circulate through channels in the stove, producing convected heat as
well as radiant heat direct from the open fire.

These designs were never patented, for being a true benefactor Franklin felt that all
men should have the benefit of his findings (Fig. 1.14).

The other inventor was Count Rumford (born Benjamin Thomson) a contemporary of
Franklin born in Massachusetts in 1753. A man of many talents, he turned his mind to
the problem of inefficient and smoking fireplaces and in 1795 published a fireplace
treatise in London called *Chimney Fireplaces with Proposals for Improving Them to Save Fuel,
to Render Dwelling Houses More comfortable and Salubrious, and Effectually to Prevent Chimneys from Smoking.*

His findings were that the throats of chimneys were too big; that stone or brick
firebacks were better than iron, as brick retains heat longer; that the sides of the fireplace should be coved; that the back of the fireplace should slant forwards towards the
throat and that smooth materials should be used to line out the fireplace walls.

He also stated that the centreline of the throat should be on the centreline of the
hearth. He believed that with chimneys in outside walls warm air went up the inside
front wall of the flue and that cold air came down the outside back wall. He therefore
proposed the smoke shelf no bigger than 100 mm (4 in) from back to front so that the
cold air currents on hitting the shelf would bounce back, mingle with the warm air

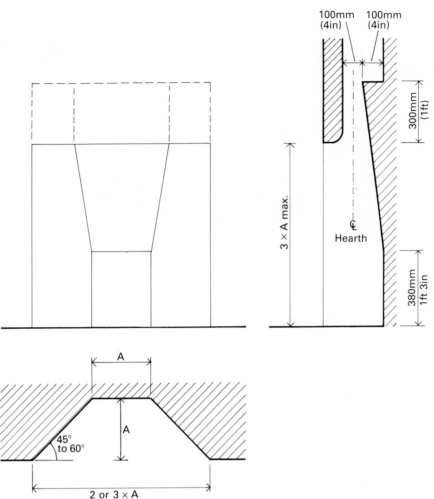

1.15 Count Rumford's recommended profile for open fireplaces 1795
This tall shallow fireplace has the centreline of the hearth and throat coinciding, with a gently sloping back rising to a narrow throat and smoke shelf, fixed well above the fireplace opening.

currents and rise again providing constant circulation, ensuring a good draught for the fire and preventing smoke entering the room. This is not, however, accepted today (see Smoke chambers on p. 59).

He laid down certain rules for the sizing of fireplace openings. He said that the back wall length should equal the depth of the hearth and that the front opening should be twice or three times the length of the back wall (making the sides slope on plan at approximately 45 – 60°). The height from the top of the hearth to the underside of the lintel should not be more than three times the depth of the fireplace.

The back wall should slope inwards about 375 mm (15 in) above the hearth and the smoke shelf should be set about 300 mm (12 in) above the underside of the lintel to the fireplace opening (Fig. 1.15).

1.16 Port Elliot, Cornwall 1804–6
The dining room fireplace designed by Sir John Soane with the Greek key pattern
incised in the jambs of the surround (*By kind permission of Country Life*).

He also advised that dampers should be used to close the chimney so that cold air
would be prevented from coming down the chimney when the fireplace was not in use.

During Count Rumford's short time in England, his masons corrected over 500
fireplaces. It soon became fashionable in London to have a fireplace which had been
overhauled by him.

After Franklin's and Rumford's inventions there were few innovations until present
times, although the fireplace continued to be decorated according to the fashion of the
day (Figs. 1.16, 1.17 and 1.18). Fireplaces tended to become smaller and more numerous. Most rooms in London houses, including servants' attics, were equipped with
fireplaces, some no more than a tiny basket. Others were hob grates, a fireplace with
space either side of the grate for keeping things warm. These resulted in a forest of
chimney stacks belching smoke into the air and contributing largely to the Dickensian
fogs which became so characteristic of Britain's city centres.

In Victorian times, cooking ranges, boilers and primitive central heating systems
were developed. Later, the open fire was equipped with a small back boiler, and so for

1.17   Standen, East Grinstead, Sussex 1891–94
        White-painted simple bold mouldings with large brick-lined fireplace designed by
        Philip Webb (*By kind permission of Country Life*).

1.18   Mains Street, Glasgow *c.* 1900
        The drawing-room fireplace of Charles Rennie Mackintosh's studio flat (*T. & R. Annan
        and Sons Ltd*).

1.19   Fallingwater, Pennsylvania, USA 1936
A large-scale fireplace designed by Frank Lloyd Wright with its rustic qualities enhanced by the stones of the site left protruding through the floor in front of the hearth (*Paul Mayen and the Western Pennsylvania Conservancy*).

the first time the open fire was put to greater use than merely heating the room in which it was situated. These boilers were improved, resulting in the high output back boiler of today which is capable of heating radiators and providing hot water for a small house.

In the early 1950s the Fuel Research Station looked into the design of open fires and found that smoke shelves and smoke chambers were not necessarily as beneficial as Count Rumford had thought. They found instead that the design of the throat and the relationship of the size of the fireplace opening to the area of the flue were critical factors in making the fire draw well. Their researches also proved that the height of the fireplace opening, whatever the size of the fire, should be kept low, ideally no more than 560–600 mm (22–24 in) above the grate.

During the 1960s and 1970s, oil-and gas-fired central heating became more widespread and the fireplace was often reduced to becoming a mere decorative device, sometimes just a repository for dried flowers or electric imitation log fires. Even some low-cost housing was equipped with district heating or warm-air or radiator systems and many houses were built without chimneys.

Suddenly, in the early 1970s, Middle Eastern oil prices rocketed and the cost of oil central heating rose dramatically. The discovery of natural gas in the North Sea eased

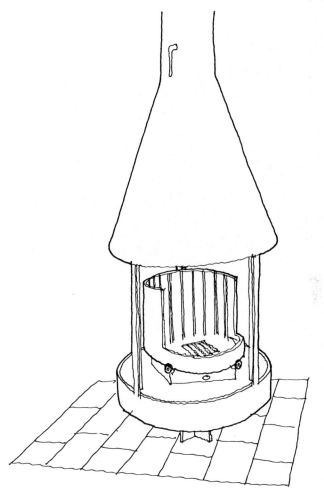

1.20   Drottningholm, Sweden 1963
      A fireplace designed for his own home by Ralph Erskine. The fireback can be revolved to
      face either the sitting or eating area of his living room (*Ralph Erskine*).

things for a time as systems were converted to gas, but the known supply of this gas is limited to little more than thirty years. There is at least 300 years supply of coal in Britain alone and so solid fuel becomes much more attractive again, which has resulted in the comeback of the open fire.

Many facts contributed to the return of the fireplace. The Clean Air Act in 1956 enforced the wider distribution of smokeless fuels, which meant that the previous objections to smoke-laden atmospheres in towns were removed. Better insulated flues and throat restrictors meant there was no need for chimneys to smoke or not to draw well. Many roomheaters and convector fires were developed which were more efficient in both fuel consumption and heat output than the traditional open fire, which wastes a large part of its heat up the chimney.

1.21 A Danish stove of about 1930 providing the central feature in an early nineteenth century house with present-day furniture (*Charlotte Baden-Powell*).

The tasks of lighting, tending and cleaning away the ashes were all jobs which, in many households, had formerly been undertaken by servants – but deep ash pits, overnight burning grates, better air controls and gas ignition all helped to make these tasks more tolerable. The low running costs and the delight of real fires are often thought to be sufficient compensation for the labour-saving ease of turning on a gas or an electric fire.

Along with the revival of solid fuel in the 1970s came the world's awareness of the serious need for conservation. Resources were seen to be running out. Electricity, to satisfy ever-increasing demand, had to be partly made with nuclear power, with all its attendant risks of radiation. There was a strong feeling that a brake should be put on the continuing rise in living standards and a deliberate nostalgia and harking back to former apparently more simple life styles was taken up by many of the middle classes. Organic food, yoga, natural materials, a need to escape the rat race– all these things were factors in getting back to the 'real' fire. People in the country began felling their own wood, made easier by the plentiful supply of dead elms, killed by an appalling epidemic of Dutch Elm disease. There was a rash of imported stoves from Europe, which were soon imitated by British manufacturers. The increase in second homes, country cottages into which to retreat from the city, gave people a chance to experience the delight and cheerfulness of an open fire, often for the first time in their lives.

Now in the 1980s we have an amazingly wide range of fireplaces from which to choose. Unlike designs for kitchens and bathrooms which inevitably are dominated by the latest technological advances in the equipment, the fireplace still offers a choice of designs ranging from the most primitive to space-age fantasies. It is possible to install a beautifully-made sophisticated appliance which will provide economical space heating as well as serve as an open fire, or alternatively to build a simple brick hearth on which to burn logs – no different in essence from medieval times and still conjuring all the magic associated with bringing one of the elements right into the home, yet taming it just sufficiently to suit our needs (Figs. 1.19, 1.20 and 1.21).

Chapter 2

THE CLEAN AIR ACTS

The Clean Air Act was introduced in 1956 and a succeeding Act followed in 1968. The purpose of these Acts was to reduce the level of air pollution, in particular the issue of 'dark' or 'black' smoke from both industrial and domestic chimneys.

These Acts empowered Local Authorities to declare Smoke Control Orders, which had to be confirmed by the Secretary of State. After the order was confirmed, six months had to elapse before the order came into operation – this six-month period allowed time for new appliances to be installed or old grates converted, which was generally aided by a local authority grant.

The effect on a householder living in a Smoke Control Area is that he is not able to burn wood or housecoal on his fires. Instead he must use one of the authorised solid fuels, gas or electricity. Oil, in itself, is not classified as a smokeless fuel, but oil-burning appliances are permitted, on the understanding that they are properly used and maintained. One exception to the prohibition of burning coal in Smoke Control Areas is to install an approved 'smoke-eating' fire or roomheater, developed by manufacturers in conjunction with the National Coal Board to burn bituminous coal smokelessly.

As Smoke Control Orders only deal with smoke from chimneys, this does not prevent people from having bonfires in the garden – providing they do not cause offence to the neighbours, who may otherwise take action to secure damages or obtain an injunction.

Before the Clean Air Acts, two smokeless zones were created: City of London and Central Manchester. It was later realised that the term was inaccurate, as it is impossible not to produce any smoke at all, so the term Smoke Control Area was substituted, although people still commonly refer to 'smokeless zones' in general conversation (Fig. 2.1).

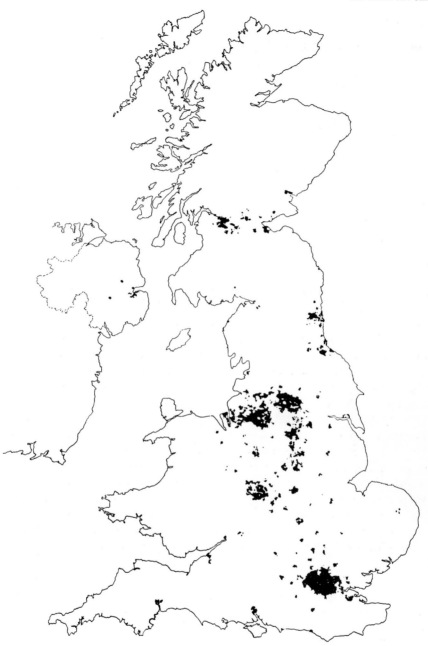

2.1   Smoke Control Areas 1977 (*Crown copyright*).

Chapter 3

FUEL

Choice of fuel

Which fuel to burn in an open fire or stove will be determined by whether or not the fire is in a Smoke Control Area, what fuels are locally available and what sort of appliance is being installed. If the appliance is in a Smoke Control Area then the choice will be limited to smokeless solid fuels. If not, then the choice can include ordinary household coal and all forms of timber. Many appliances will burn more than one sort of fuel, but some are specifically designed to burn only one or two types. It is vital that the right type and the right size of fuel be used in order to gain optimum efficiency. Manufacturers' instructions should always be adhered to when selecting fuels, alternatively seek the advice of the local coal merchant.

As a guide to the comparative efficiency of fuels see Table 3.1. Note that the costs relate to the efficiency of the appliance and are therefore the relative useful cost per kWh.

Coal merchants

Nearly 90 per cent of solid fuel in the UK, including all natural coal, is produced by the National Coal Board. The remainder is manufactured by independent firms or imported. In order to buy coal from the NCB, coal merchants must be members of the Approved Coal Merchants' Scheme.

This is an independent body which grades coal merchants into three categories. The lowest grade, a dealer, will only have to fulfill very basic requirements regarding his premises, hours of business and range of fuels and will generally sell for cash only. The second and most universally used category is the Approved Coal Merchant. He must have a proper order office, carry on trade throughout all times of the year and be able to provide basic technical advice about choice of fuels. The third and smallest top-class

Table 3.1 Comparative Fuel Costs in 1982

Fuel	Appliance	Typical thermal efficiency (%)	Relative average cost per useful kWh
Natural gas	Flued radiant fire	55	1.00
Electricity night store heating	Storage heater	98	1.03
Bulk propane gas	Flueless radiant fixed fire	98	1.18
Oil	Boiler	75	1.49
Smokeless solid fuel	Closed fire	60	1.50
Paraffin	Roomheater	98	1.56
Cylinder propane gas	Flueless radiant fixed fire	98	1.90
Electricity domestic tariff	Electric fire	100	2.60
Smokeless solid fuel	Open fire	30	2.71

NB: The costs do not take account of any standing charges.

category is the Diploma Coal Merchant. He must have premises open to the public, with staff fully trained to answer the public's questions about both fuel and appliances. He would normally have quite a few appliances on display and be able to give general information about appliances which he does not have in stock (Fig. 3.1).

3.1   Coal merchant symbols.

Solid fuel

Solid fuel comes in three categories – bituminous coal, natural smokeless and manufactured smokeless. On the whole, smokeless fuels will give out up to one-third more heat than the equivalent weight in naturally occurring coal, but they are more expensive and the lighter smokeless fuels take up nearly twice the space to store than coal and the denser solid fuels. (See fuel storage pages 30–3).

Some manufactured smokeless fuels have been carbonised. These are natural coals which are crushed and baked to drive off most of the volatile matter. The resulting porous-looking hot coke is cooled by quenching with water. Variations in the type of coal and the temperatures used result in different sorts of manufactured smokeless fuels. These fuels vary in their calorific values, as shown in Table 3.2. Price is not necessarily reflected by the heat content as transport costs are a large part of the cost, so consumers who have appliances which will take a choice of fuels would be well advised to buy a fuel with the highest calorific value for the lowest cost.

Housecoal comes from the bituminous group of British coals. It ignites easily and burns with a bright flame and comes in three qualities, Groups 1, 2 and 3. Group 1 is the most expensive coal which comes in a variety of sizes; the larger sized cobbles are suitable for open fires and large nuts (trebles) or nuts (doubles) for room heaters.

Housecoal is not suitable for Smoke Control Areas, unless burnt in appliances designed to burn coal smokelessly such as the Rayburn Prince. For use outside Smoke Control Areas, housecoal is generally best value for money.

Table 3.2 Typical Calorific Value of Solid Fuels

Fuel types	kJ/kg	Btu/lb
Anthracite	33 500	14 400
Welsh dry steam coal	33 100	14 200
Phurnacite	30 900	13 300
Housecoal	29 000	12 500
Coalite	27 900	12 000
Rexco	27 900	12 000
Sunbrite	26 800	11 500

Welsh Dry Steam Coal is a natural smokeless coal suitable for use in either improved open fires or closed appliances. It burns slowly with a bright flame and has a high calorific output – large or small nuts are often used in boilers.

Anthracite is a non-bituminous very old type of coal and is the best-known natural smokeless fuel. It is dense and slow-burning, ideal for stoves and boilers. It comes in six sizes from grains, beans, peas, stovesse and stovenuts up to the largest size French nuts. The three smallest sizes are used for gravity feed stoves and boilers.

Housewarm is a specially-selected grade of natural bituminous coal to be used in some fan-assisted smoke-reducing appliances where it burns smokelessly and therefore can be used in Smoke Control Areas.

Homefire is a manufactured smokeless fuel. It comes in hexagonal shapes and is designed to give all the best features of housecoal, but without smoke. Easy to light, it burns for long periods with a good flame and great heat.

Coalite is a manufactured carbonised fuel, being coal which has been 'baked' in large

3.2 Solid fuels: (*Solid Fuel Advisory Service*):
(a) Housecoal   (e) Coalite
(b) Welsh dry steam coal   (f) Rexco
(c) Anthracite   (g) Phurnacite
(d) Homefire   (h) Sunbrite

ovens to make it smokeless. It is a light fuel, burns well with a clean flame and is suitable for most stoves, cookers and boilers.

NCC Rexco Limited manufacture four carbonised smokeless fuels which are light in weight and burn with a good flame:

Rexco   suitable for open fires
Royal   suitable for open fires
Rexco Nuts suitable for roomheaters and boilers
Superbrite suitable for roomheaters and boilers

Phurnacite is a very dense hard manufactured smokeless fuel, slow burning and clean to use – and it comes in ovoid shapes with two grooves. It is produced from Welsh dry steam coal but has the characteristics of anthracite and burns well in stoves, boilers and cookers.

Sunbrite is a manufactured carbonised fuel which is denser than others, so is only suitable for closed appliances or for fan-assisted or underfloor draught open fires. Sunbrite doubles are for roomheaters, open fires and large boilers; singles are for smaller boilers.

Coke is a fuel no longer manufactured. It was a coal which had been through a dry distillation process to take off the volatile constituents which made up town gas. The gas coke industry has disappeared since the arrival of natural gas.

Fireglo is an imported fuel generally for boilers and cookers, except the heat storage type.

Extracite is an imported fuel which has similar characteristics and uses as Phurnacite. Other manufactured fuels are sometimes available, but not all are regarded as smokeless (Fig. 3.2).

Wood as fuel

Wood, when reasonably dry, has slightly less than half the calorific value of coal, but is less than half the price.

It is important that wood is well dried before being put on the fire. Freshly cut 'green' wood contains over 50 per cent water. It takes six to twelve months for this level to be reduced to an acceptable 20 per cent. Well-dried wood will show radial cracks at the sawn ends. Wet wood when burned will leave tar deposits in the flue which, if allowed to build up, can eventually catch fire and become a fire hazard.

In fireplaces where new softwood is burnt continually, the flue should be swept several times a year to minimise the risk of fire.

Softwoods burn faster and less efficiently than hardwoods, but weight for weight their calorific output is similar, so a larger storage area and more refuelling time is needed for softwood. Hardwoods are more satisfactory as they take longer to burn. Poplar and willow give out less heat than oak, ash or beech which are considered the prime woods for burning. Resinous softwoods like pine tend to spit, but make the best

Table 3.3 Typical calorific values of firewoods and peat

Wood	Moisture Content approx %	Gross Calorific Value as fired	
		KJ/Kg	Btu/lb
Beech	30–40	11,900–14,000	5,100–6,000
Douglas fir	35	14,000	6,000
Fir – common	35	12,800–13,700	5,500–5,900
Hemlock	50–60	7,900– 9,800	3,400–4,200
Oak – red	30–35	12,600–13,500	5,400–5,800
Peat – briquettes	10–14	18,100–19,800	7,800–8,500
Peat	25–40	12,600–17,500	5,400–7,500
Pine – bark	40–50	11,000–13,300	4,750–5,700
Pine – white	40	12,400	5,350
Pine – yellow	35	14,500	6,250
Redwood	50	10,500	4,500
Sawdust		17,500–18,600	7,500–8,000
Spruce – bark	60	8,400	3,600
Western red cedar	30	15,800	6,800
Willow	60	7,700	3,300

Extracted from Table 45 of the *Energy Users' Databook* edited by H B Locke and published by Graham & Trotman Ltd London 1981

kindling. Elm contains a lot of moisture when cut and needs a good twelve months to dry out. Holly is dense and burns well, apple has a marvellous smell. Table 3.3 illustrates the calorific values of various firewoods and peat.

Firewood sources

Wood can be bought from timber merchants and the Forestry Commission. It can also sometimes be bought from tree surgeons, contract gardeners, Local Authority Parks Departments (who fell their own trees), demolition sites and sawmills (who sell offcuts).

Wood can also be gathered by hand. On common land it is permissible to collect fallen dead wood.

Wood is sold either by the tonne or in 'cords'. A cord is made up of a pile 8 × 4 × 4 ft (2.4 × 1.2 × 1.2 m) or 128 ft³ (3.6 m³).

When one is buying wood for a wood-burning stove, it is possible to order logs cut to length to suit the size of the firebox. This is obviously worth doing in order to pack the stove most efficiently and to reduce the intervals between refuelling.

Recycling newspapers

Old newspapers can be made into logs or bricks as a useful, if time-consuming way, of using them up. There are *paper log rollers* (Fig. 3.3) which are designed to roll the paper very tightly. The logs are best soaked in water or even a few inches of waste oil to break down the fibres, and then left to dry out before burning.

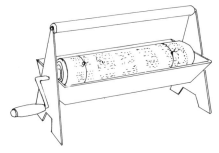

3.3   Newspaper log roller.

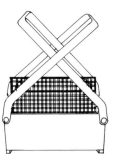

3.4   Newspaper brick press.

There are also *paper brick presses* (Fig. 3.4) which compress sodden newspapers into rectangular bricks – when dry these will give roughly half the calorific value of anthracite, with about 2 per cent ash content and very little soot or smoke.

All these devices take up a lot of time and energy and will not make great savings as the manufacturers claim, but form a satisfying way of getting rid of old papers.

Fuel storage

The type of fuel chosen to burn will determine the size of store needed coupled with availability or otherwise of having several fuel deliveries a year. A fire which burns little but softwood will need several tonnes, and therefore several deliveries a year, while a stove burning a dense smokeless fuel may get by on as little as 1.5 tonnes a year.

As a rough guide for storage areas, the table below gives the comparative sizes of fuel per cubic metre (m^3):

carbonised fuels : 2.24 m^3 per tonne (78 ft^3 per ton)
softwood   : 1.60 m^3 per tonne (56 ft^3 per ton)
hardwood   : 1.33 m^3 per tonne (46 ft^3 per ton)
dense fuel   : 1.27 m^3 per tonne (44 ft^3 per ton)

Storing wood

Timber should be stacked, preferably in the open but under cover from direct rain and snow, to allow it to dry out properly before burning. Stacking wood inside sheds will not enable it to dry out well unless there is really good permanent cross-ventilation. Bringing the wood into the house from the outside stack, a day or two before it is needed, should be enough to dry off any surface moisture on the bark.

Large logs are better split, as they then burn more easily. Small logs may be split with an axe, larger ones will need steel wedges and a 12 lb hammer. Some softwoods will need splitting with a small cleaver to make kindling. As all this sort of activity is almost inevitable when burning wood, plan to have the wood-splitting area adjacent to the store, preferably under cover with a good solid dry floor with space for a saw horse and a place to hang the tools – i.e. chain saw, bowsaw, axe, hammer, hand cleaver and wedges. Remember that far bigger storage areas will be needed for timber, compared with solid fuels.

As a guide to timber consumption, a woodstove burning 13.5 kg (30 lb) of softwood a day for the six-month cold season will burn about 2.5 tonnes which would need a volume of 4 m^3 (140 ft^3). Open fires will burn much more wood than a closed stove and may need storage for 6 m^3 (210 ft^3) for a six-month supply.

Large log baskets will be needed to carry the wood into the house and smaller containers for kindling and newspaper.

Storing solid fuel

Carbonised smokeless fuels are much lighter than coal and other non-carbonised smokeless fuels and therefore need more space. The Coal Board recommends a minimum storage capacity of 2.7 m^3 (95 ft^3) for light fuels and 1.27 m^3 (45 ft^3) for dense fuel. As this figure represents only about six weeks supply for a small house, this volume should be greatly increased if the economy and labour-saving expenditure of bulk buying in the summer is to be practised and indeed encouraged.

The fuel store should be accessible from the house under cover and should not be too far away from the appliance it has to serve. If the fuel store is within the house then it should be accessible from a lobby, store or utility room. The store should not be more than 45 m (148 ft) carrying distance from the delivery lorry.

Delivery lorries ideally need 1.2 m (4 ft) clear either side for the coalman to lift off the sacks of coal and if the housing is in a cul-de-sac then a turning circle of 17 m (56 ft) is required. Passages and corridors leading from the vehicle to the store must be a minimum of 900 mm (3 ft) wide and 2.29 m (7 ft 6 in) high. The width of the passage should be increased to 1.45 m (4 ft 9 in) at right-angles to the fuel store doors, to allow the coalman to tip the sack over his shoulder into the store. Chutes and hoppers, unless very large, are not as good as open access, as it is difficult to fit the mouth of the coal sack into them and some fuel will be spilt.

Fuel stores located outside can sometimes be incorporated with dustbin stores – remember that dustmen have similar vehicle and access problems as coal merchants. Fuel stores can also be housed in the ends of large garages, preferably with separate doors from the side, so that access either for delivery or for the householder is not

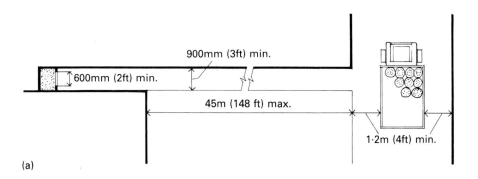

900mm (3ft) min.

600mm (2ft) min.

45m (148 ft) max.

1·2m (4ft) min.

(a)

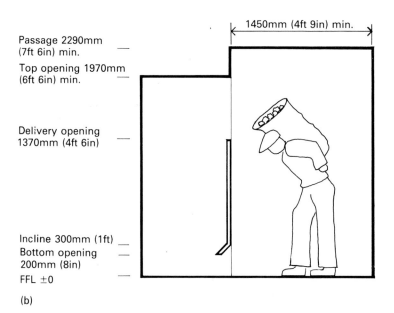

1450mm (4ft 9in) min.

Passage 2290mm (7ft 6in) min. —

Top opening 1970mm (6ft 6in) min. —

Delivery opening 1370mm (4ft 6in) —

Incline 300mm (1ft) —
Bottom opening 200mm (8in) —

FFL ±0 —

(b)

3.5   Solid fuel storage
(a) fuel store access
(b) fuel store dimensions.

obstructed when the car is in the garage.

Prefabricated concrete bunkers can be bought in various sizes and are suitable for external use — but they do look fairly hideous. But shop around for one or two newer neater-looking lightweight bunkers.

When constructing the fuel store, only good strong materials should be used as they will get rough treatment. The opening to the fuel store should preferably be the full width of the store and never smaller than 600 mm (2 ft) wide. The top of the fuel-retaining board should be 1.37 m (4 ft 6 in) above floor level with an opening above of not less than 600 mm (2 ft) high. The fuel-retaining board can either be designed as a hopper with gap at the bottom allowing the coal to be shovelled out into scuttles, or with a series of boards slotted into channels, which are removed one by one as the pile of fuel descends (Fig. 3.5). This last method may be easier to fill hods quickly but is probably less dust-free. When, in the latter system, the coal cellar is filled from a coal hole in the pavement above, it is important to replace all the boards before the coal merchant arrives, otherwise fuel will gush onto the area floor when the door is opened and it is then impossible to reinsert the boards without emptying half the fuel.

Fuel stores should be made safe against housebreakers if delivery access is from outside and house access from inside.

Coal hods or scuttles and shovels will be needed to carry the fuel from the store to the appliance and a place to store them will be needed if an open fire or stove is not in use during the summer months.

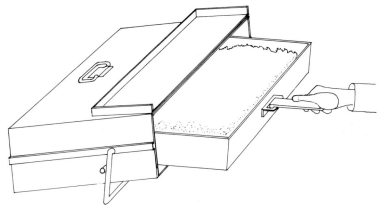

3.6   Ash carrier
Dustfree method of emptying ash from open fires and roomheaters, in three sizes to suit different widths of ashpan (by Winchwing).

Ash disposal

Ash disposal must be considered along with fuel storage. Metal dustbins will be needed for hot ashes. Alternatively a small portable metal bin can be used for carrying the hot ashes out and storing until cold enough to place in plastic bins or bags. These bins, commonly called 'ash tidies', will hold an average of three ashpans before having to be emptied. Their advantage over an ordinary bucket and shovel is that they trap the ash at source and prevent it flying about when being emptied or carried through the house (Fig. 3.6).

Wood ash may be saved for use on the compost heap or scattered directly (when cool) as a fertiliser for the ground in spring.

Lighting a fire

One traditional way to light an open fire is to start with lightly crumpled sheets of newspaper, surrounded by a 'wigwam' heap of dry kindling or sticks. Around this small coals, charred wood from the previous fire, or small dry logs are then stacked. This pile should be kept to the back of the grate and the newspaper lit in two or three places at the bottom. As the initial flames burn-up the paper, the kindling may collapse and need rearranging, so it is generally a good idea to stay watching the fire at least until the larger pieces ignite. As the fire proceeds, so larger logs and lumps of coal can be added.

As the logs burn down they will need occasional rearranging in order to bring the lit surfaces together again – keeping a fire or, indeed, a bonfire alight is a matter of allowing enough air in underneath for combustion, yet still keeping the fuel fairly tightly packed to allow the flames to move around the maximum surface area. Wet fuel is impossible to burn when a fire is being started but, once a really good red hot fire bed is established, it will eventually ignite, after sizzling and giving off a lot of steam and generally slowing down the fire.

Where fires are difficult to light, perhaps because of a very cold wet flue, or fuel which is not sufficiently dry, then chemical firelighters are a convenient alternative to either gas or electric ignition. They can be used in Smoke Control Areas, getting rid of the need for paper and kindling and are a great help for lighting smokeless fuels.

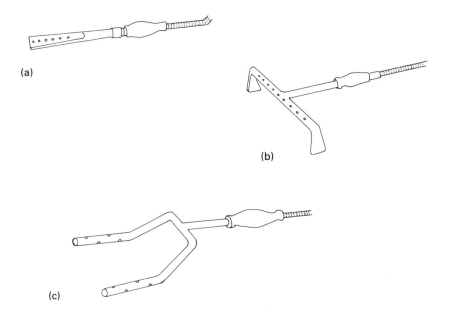

(a)

(b)

(c)

3.7   Gas pokers
    (a) blade poker for small openings in stoves
    (b) T-shaped poker for open fires and roomheaters
    (c) two-pronged poker for open fires (by Baxi).

Gas pokers and burners

With the introduction of the Clean Air Act, and the subsequent need to burn smokeless fuels in Smoke Control Areas, it is highly desirable to have gas ignition to start a fire of smokeless fuels. Not only are they harder to ignite than wood and ordinary coal which have a far higher volatile content, but the burning of kindling and paper itself will cause smoke, which may be allowed by a Local Authority, but generally only if no gas is available.

Many appliances incorporate gas ignition, but where these are not available then there are two types of *gas poker*: One is a blade type of poker, most suitable for stoves and boilers – the other is a 'T'-shaped poker with jets emerging from the 'T' bar which is more suitable for open fires and roomheaters (Fig. 3.7). A gas cock will be needed adjacent to the hearth and this should have a removable key where young children are around which, if removed, prevents a child turning on the poker when it is not lit. Where there is no mains gas, then the poker can be attached to a small portable gas cylinder.

Gas pokers and burners should conform to BS 3328: 1961 which deals with aerated and non-aerated single blade pokers, non-aerated burners inserted beneath the bottom grate and ignition burners for open fires with deep ashpits.

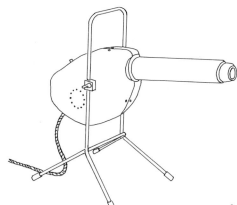

3.8   Electric firelighter (by Pifco).

Electric firelighters

An alternative to gas ignition is to light the fire with an *electric firelighter* (Fig. 3.8). This will need a 13A socket outlet positioned near the hearth. The nozzle of the firelighter is placed into the fuel and it blows very hot air at about 800 °C (1500 °F) without smoke or flame to ignite the fire. When the fire is lit, the heat switch is turned off and a cold air stream then fans the fire and helps to cool the body of the firelighter. A safety switch is incorporated to prevent young children from turning it on accidentally.

Chapter 4

FIREPLACE DESIGN

Professional advice

Installing a new fireplace is not cheap. The prices of manufactured fireplaces range from about £100 to £1000 in 1983, depending upon the type of appliance chosen. This is for the appliance alone and does not include installation costs.

It therefore makes sense to take some advice. Initially, information about appliances and solid fuels can be obtained from the Solid Fuel Advisory Service (SFAS) and, if it is just a matter of exchanging an old grate for a new one, then a competent builder may be all that is required; but if a new chimney is to be built or the fireplace is to be as well designed as a good kitchen or bathroom, then it is advisable to employ an architect. Names and addresses of local architects and the scale of charges can be obtained from the Royal Institute of British Architects (RIBA). Architects will advise on appliances, design purpose-made fireplaces, draw up plans and specifications obtaining any necessary approvals, get estimates from building contractors and supervise the work during construction.

Consents

Installing a fireplace that works efficiently can be complicated. The Building Regulations regarding the construction of hearths and chimneys are stringent – rightly so – as they are designed to prevent structures falling down and to safeguard the house from catching fire. When a new chimney is built or a fireplace installed where no previous fireplace existed, then approval is needed from the Local Authority Building Inspector (or the District Surveyor in the GLC area). He will not only have to approve the proposals in advance but will also inspect the work as it proceeds to ensure that it is, in fact, built according to the regulations. For a summary of the Building Regulations see pages 131–52.

If a new chimney is added to an old house, or an existing chimney is raised, then planning permission may be required. This is more likely if the house is in a *conservation area* or if it is *listed* as a *historic building*, in which case the advice of the Local Planning Authority should be sought.

Location of the fireplace

When planning a fireplace for a new house, or for a house without a chimney, the position of the fireplace should be carefully considered. Is it to be focus of family life – the place around which friends and relations will gather?

Will it also do a double job of heating hot water and radiators? If so, then the plumbing connections and short lengths of pipe runs will dictate the position.

Is the chimney stack to serve other rooms, either with back-to-back hearths or fireplaces in upper storeys? In this case, the position of the stack will be conditioned by the planning of the rooms.

A chimney on an inside wall will save up to 25 per cent of heat compared with a chimney placed on an outside wall. On the other hand, the chimney on the outside wall of a new house may save on foundation costs. It can also have a soot door and ash pan accessible from outside or even have a fireplace on the outside to serve a courtyard.

For some houses, close to tall buildings, the position of the fireplace may be dictated by the position of the flue, which should be placed as far away as possible from these objects, to avoid downdraughts.

Most fireplaces are placed in the living room, but it makes sense to have the fireplace in the room where the family gathers most. This can sometimes be the kitchen. If the kitchen is large enough to contain a fireplace as well as all the other equipment, then it could also double for some of the cooking with swing-out grills, rotisseries or pot-hanging cranes suspended over the fire.

Cross-circulation

Having decided on the basic location of the fireplace, then make sure that it is not positioned between two doors, which would create cross-circulation between people sitting in front of the fire. It is also best not to have any opening doors or windows immediately adjacent to the fireplace, as these could cause cross-currents and adversely affect the draught.

Seating

The fireplace should be positioned so that a maximum number of people can sit round the fire. Backs of seats should ideally not be further than 3 m (10 ft) from the face of the fire. Seats at the side of a fire need to be nearer than seats opposite the fire to feel the benefit of the heat. Of course, if the room has some other additional heating, then this factor is not quite so critical, but seats still need to be reasonably close to one another for people to be able to talk comfortably. It is therefore best if fireplaces have spaces on both sides and in front, in which seating can be arranged. They are therefore preferably not placed in corners of rooms but along a wall or brought out into a large room, either freestanding or within a room divider.

Television

Planning a living room is difficult because of the duality created between the rival attractions of the fireplace and the television. Obviously the arrangement of seats must be fairly permanent, as it is inconvenient to keep moving heavy furniture around. The solution most often adopted is to place the television alongside the fireplace, often incorporating a place for it within the design of the fireplace wall, so that both fireplace and television can be viewed from most of the chairs. Alternatively if the main seats are placed at right-angles to the fireplace then the television can be positioned opposite the fireplace and still be viewed by most of the seats surrounding the fire.

Ventilation

One of the great merits of the open fire is that it provides natural ventilation as it draws air up the chimney. However, this ventilation can be distinctly uncomfortable with a roaring fire creating draughts all round the back of the room. To prevent too much air rushing up the chimney, a throat restrictor should be fitted (see page 57) the benefit of which can be seen in the following table which shows the air flow from a room in normal living conditions, with open solid-fuel fires when connected to a 225 mm (9 in) square flue in a two-storey house. Open fires with underfloor air supplied from outside the room only marginally reduce the ventilating effect; but their main advantage is to make starting the fire much easier.

Open fire with unrestricted throat	200 m³ (7000 ft³) per hour
Open fire with underfloor air supply and unrestricted throat	160 m³ (5500 ft³) per hour.
Open fire with restricted throat	100 m³ (3500 ft³) per hour

Open fires need air passing over them to ensure that the products of combustion are carried up the flue. Insufficient air may cause the smoke to blow back into the room. The Building Regulations require that there is sufficient combustion air for the efficient operation of the fireplace appliance. In practice, natural leakage around doors and windows and an openable window are usually considered sufficient for appliances rated up to 12 kW (41 000 Btu/h) but in modern, well-insulated, close-carpeted houses, this might be a problem. A louvre over the door or a floor grille close to the hearth may be all that is needed. If no other air inlet is supplied, then the door should not be draught-proofed, because a 1 mm gap all around the edges of a door will give about 60 cm² (9 in²) of ventilation.

Where there is an open fireplace within a kitchen which is fitted with an extract fan, an air inlet, remote from the fan, should be provided to prevent the lowering of the room pressure drawing fumes from the chimney back into the kitchen.

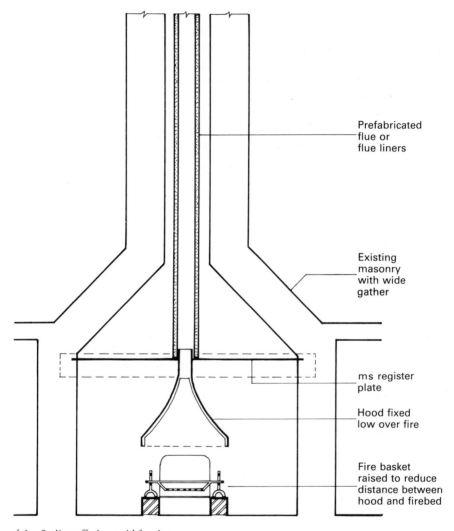

Prefabricated flue or flue liners

Existing masonry with wide gather

ms register plate

Hood fixed low over fire

Fire basket raised to reduce distance between hood and firebed

4.1   Sealing off a large old fireplace.

Design considerations

Size of fireplace

The fireplace should be designed to be in scale with the room. A baronial hall type of fireplace looks ridiculous in a small low-ceilinged room. Similarly, a small fireplace within a large room will not only look insignificant but may not give out enough heat.

Style of fireplace

Fireplaces can now be bought in any style imaginable, whether it be early Gothic, Spanish colonial, fifties functional or 'high-tech', as the fireplace has always been decorated to portray the image the family wishes to have of itself. Sadly this can bring out heights of extravagant vulgarity which have to be seen to be believed. However, it *is* possible, with a bit of diligent searching, to find well-designed 'off-the-peg' modern fireplaces or faithful reproductions of earlier styles. The alternative, of course, is to have the fireplace purpose-made to a particular design.

Although many people would argue that the fireplace should reflect the style in which the house was built, many current designs look extremely well in old settings. However, if an old fireplace exists which has the merit of being pleasingly designed, then resist the impulse to tear it out. Such a fireplace adds a genuine interest to the room, along with the mouldings of the cornices and architraves, and if the room is all of one piece, changing the fireplace would be a loss. It is often possible to change the grate, add a throat restrictor or even insert a whole new firebox in order to make the fireplace more efficient.

Old fireplaces in large recesses

It is quite common in old houses and cottages to find a very large fireplace recess, sometimes as big as 3 × 2 m (10 ft × 6 ft 8 in) in which stands on open fire. With such a recess it is also common to find that there is a large chimney overhead with an enormous gather from the top of the recess with the result that most of the heat of the fire is lost up the chimney and tremendous draughts are created in the room. Two things can alleviate this problem – one is to line the flue, both to reduce the size and to insulate the chimney against the cold – and the second is to put in a false ceiling at the bottom of the flue liner, with a hood suspended from the ceiling down over the open fire. The hood reduces the height of the fire opening and helps to gather the smoke into the flue rather than back into the room (Fig. 4.1).

Central freestanding fireplaces

The central fireplace is an attractive idea, much loved by contemporary designers. It is particularly suitable for a large living room where it can be the central feature. It is also often associated with youth hostels where, reminiscent of the camp fire, a large number of people can gather round to sing songs and tell stories.

Such fireplaces are, however, beset with functional problems. They are extremely susceptible to draughts created by cross-currents from doors and windows opening on opposite sides of the room. Also, unless installed in a single-storey building, it may be difficult to accommodate the chimney within the rooms above. As with all fireplaces, the relationship between the fireplace opening and the flue is critical. The central fireplace, by definition, has an opening all round and will therefore need a much larger diameter to get anywhere near the desirable 1:8 relationship of flue and fireplace opening. It is therefore essential to keep the opening size to a minimum and this is best achieved by raising the hearth and suspending a hood low over the hearth.

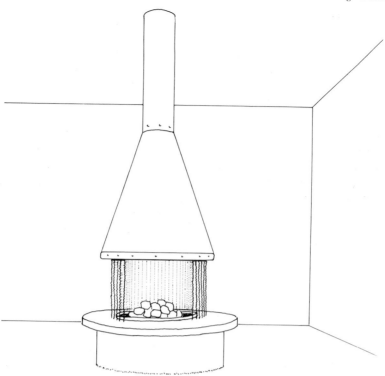

4.2   Central fireplace with fire curtain ('Central Canopy' by Bell).

The hearth should extend well outside the grate to contain the ash and to prevent people standing too close. The hearth should incorporate an underfloor air duct and draught control and be fitted with a deep ashpit.

The hood will get very hot and unless well insulated should, if made in metal, be double skinned to provide an air gap.

Another device which can usually reduce the effects of cross-currents to a central fireplace is to suspend a mesh fire curtain from the edge of the hood which can be drawn round to suit the draughts and also act as a spark guard (Fig. 4.2).

A simpler way to take the guesswork out of the central fireplace is to install a free-standing appliance, which in fact will not have an opening all round, but will have a far greater chance of burning successfully and, if it incorporates doors, will keep the fire in when unattended.

Opening up a fireplace

Many houses have fireplaces which have been blocked up. Sometimes the surround is still there and the opening has simply been fitted with a panel covering the opening. In this case, removing the panel may simply reveal the fireplace still intact. But if the whole surround has been taken out and the opening bricked up, then much more work will be involved. The bricks or blocks will have to be removed to reveal the arch or lintel of the fireplace opening. The flue should be swept and the interior of the flue inspected for any leaks by means of a smoke test. The pot may also need renewing and the rendering and flaunching to the chimney stack repairing.

Depending upon what sort and size of fireplace or roomheater is to be installed, the opening may need enlarging, which may mean inserting a new constructional lintel or throat-forming lintel (see page 56). If the gather to the flue is badly formed, then this may also need to be rebuilt and it is always advisable to fit a throat restrictor in the flue for an open fire, as this will increase the amount of heat directed into the room. If a roomheater or stove is to be installed which will stand in front of the chimney breast, then the hearth may need to be extended to comply with modern building regulations (see pages 135–40).

Fireplace plans

When a fireplace is being designed for a new building, the choices for positioning the fire are numerous; listed below are the various alternatives:

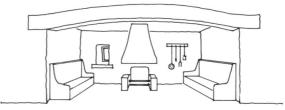

4.3   Fireplace within seating recess.

4.4   'Jøtul 6' wood-burning stove in Welsh farmhouse fireplace (*Charlotte Baden-Powell*).

Fireplace within seating recess (Fig. 4.3) This is the traditional farmhouse plan with the fireplace within a large recess some 3 m (10 ft) wide × 1.5 m (5 ft) deep which allows enough room for seating on either side. A variation of this type is illustrated in Fig. 4.4 where the space either side of the fire is used for fuel.

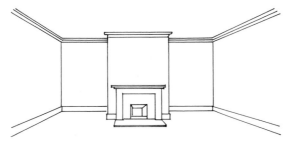

4.5   Fireplace on internal chimney breast.

Fireplace on internal chimney breast (Fig. 4.5) This is the most common position for a fireplace. Here the chimney breast projects into the room, and is best positioned in the middle of a wall to allow for maximum seating area all round the fire.

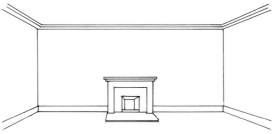

4.6   Fireplace on external chimney breast.

Fireplace on external chimney breast (Fig. 4.6) This is similar to the previous fireplace (Fig. 4.5) but has the chimney breast projecting externally. This enables the fireplace to be fitted flush into the surrounding wall.

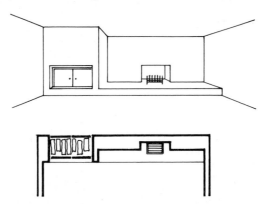

4.7   Fireplace with pass-through fuel store.

Fireplace design

Fireplace with pass-through fuel store (Fig. 4.7) Here the fireplace is situated on an external wall with a fuel store cupboard positioned alongside, making it easy to replace the fuel from outside, thus avoiding bringing dust through the house. It also dispenses with the need for coal scuttles and baskets.

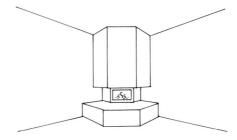

4.8   Fireplace in internal corner.

Fireplace in internal corner (Fig. 4.8) Corner fireplaces look nice and snug but are not as good for a large number of seats as a fireplace placed centrally along a wall.

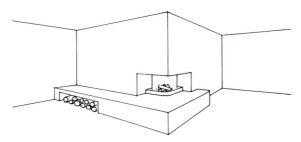

4.9   Fireplace on external corner.

Fireplace on external corner (Fig. 4.9) This is an excellent position for a large 'L'-shaped room, as it provides a central focus for the room and allows for a lot of seating on either side.

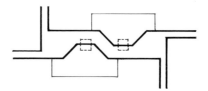

4.10   Side-by-side fireplaces.

Side-by-side fireplaces (Fig. 4.10) Side-by-side fireplaces must have separate flues but can share the same chimney stack. Here the plan shows fireplaces serving a living room on one side and a barbecue for an adjacent courtyard.

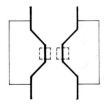

4.11   Back-to-back fireplaces.

Back-to-back fireplaces (Fig. 4.11) Fireplaces placed back-to-back must have separate flues but can share the same chimney stack while serving separate rooms.

Central chimney stacks have the advantage over external wall stacks of conserving heat within the house, but have the disadvantage of not being able to have externally accessible ash pits and it is not so easy to provide them with underfloor fresh air inlets.

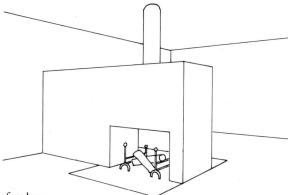

4.12   Two-way fireplace.

Two-way fireplace (Fig. 4.12) A fireplace acting as a room divider with openings on two sides so that the fire can be enjoyed from both sides of the room.

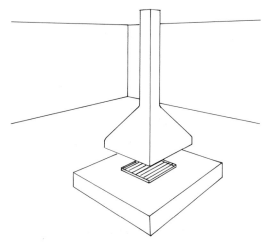

4.13   Central freestanding fireplace.

Central freestanding fireplace (Fig. 4.13) A fireplace standing in or near the middle of a room. Care must be taken with the design to ensure proper functioning (see page 40).

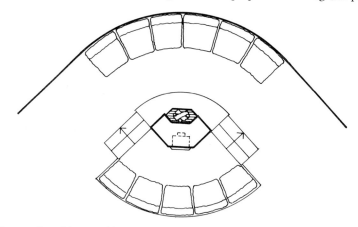

4.14   Freestanding chimney with seating, back-to-back with TV viewing.

Freestanding chimney with TV viewing (Fig. 4.14) This plan shows a fireplace set in a freestanding chimney, back-to-back with a seating area for watching television. This plan successfully avoids the problem of trying to reconcile the two foci of fireplace and television, but a large room is needed to accommodate two areas of seating.

Fireplace types

The location of the fireplace within the house having been decided, the next consideration is which type of fireplace to install. Below are listed the main basic types of fireplace. For more information about these fireplaces, see Chapters 10 and 11 on fireplace appliances and surrounds.

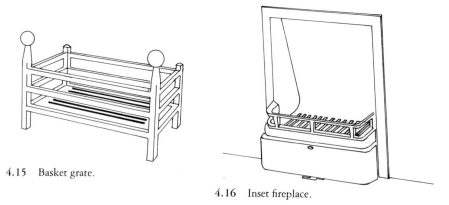

4.15   Basket grate.

4.16   Inset fireplace.

Basket grate (Fig. 4.15) Basket grates sit upon a hearth within a chimney recess. To obtain a good draught, a hood or glass panel will be needed to reduce the gap between the top of the basket and the underside of the flue.

Inset fireplace (Fig. 4.16) These are proprietary fireplaces designed to be built into the chimney breast and can usually be supplied with back boilers for central heating and domestic hot water. They are sometimes sold together with the surround.

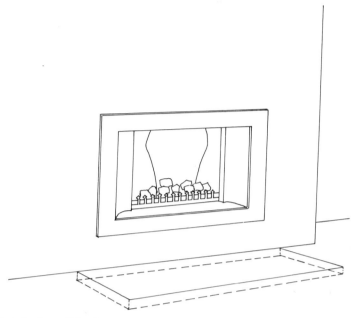

4.17 Hole-in-the-wall fireplace.

Hole-in-the-wall fireplace (Fig. 4.17) This is a fire raised off the floor, recessed into a chimney breast so that it looks like a hole in the wall. A hearth is still required and this is sometimes designed as a raised seat with the space underneath used as a log store.

4.18 Underfloor draught fire (Baxi Burnall) within stone arch (*Baxi Heating*).

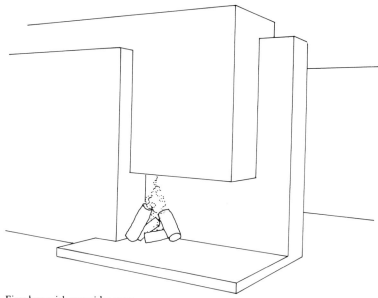

4.19   Fireplace with two sides open.

Fireplace with two sides open (Fig. 4.19) This design is popular on the Continent and in Scandinavia and is sometimes known as a 'Swedish hearth'. Here the front and the sides of the fire are open, exposing more of the fire to the room and needing cantilevered masonry or a steel hood suspended above.

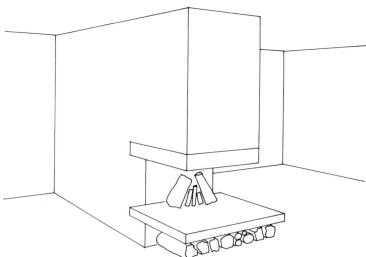

4.20   Fireplace with three sides open.

Fireplace with three sides open (Fig. 4.20) Similar to the previous fireplace (Fig. 4.19), but with three sides open. This is suitable for an island situation or for a peninsular wall between two rooms.

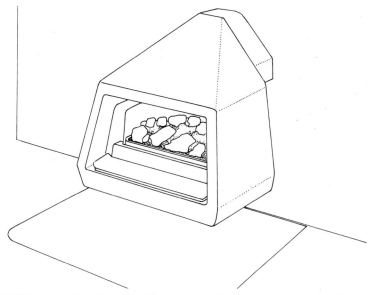

4.21   Wall-hung fireplace ('Acorn' by Ocees) in enamelled, copper or aluminium finishes.

Wall-hung fireplace (Fig. 4.21) Proprietary fireplaces, usually with steel casing, designed to be hung from the chimney breast wall.

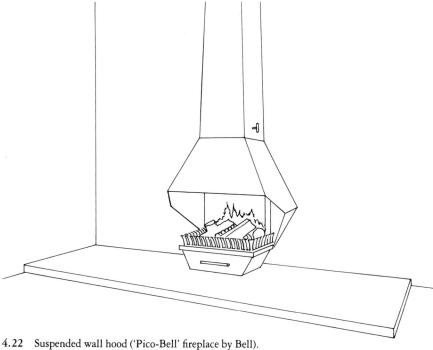

4.22   Suspended wall hood ('Pico-Bell' fireplace by Bell).

4.23   Suspended ceiling hood ('Jalco Traditional' by Wonderfire).

Suspended hoods (Figs. 4.22 & 4.23) Steel hoods suspended from the wall or ceiling over a raised hearth. The hearth is often extended to provide fireside seating.

4.24   Freestanding stove ('Petit Godin' by Ellis Sykes).

4.25　Freestanding studio stove (by Trianco Redfyre) with slate hearth and mirrors in back of fireplace recess giving the illusion of a two-way fireplace (*Charlotte Baden-Powell*).

Freestanding stove (Figs. 4.24 & 4.25) A stove placed on a hearth in front of a chimney breast. Adjacent space will be needed for a fuel hod, ash bins and tools. A soot door in the chimney breast may be needed to sweep the flue.

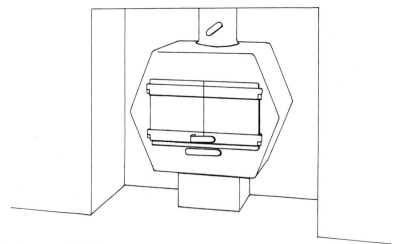

4.26   Stove set within chimney recess ('Marlborough' woodburning stove by Logfires).

Recessed stove (Fig. 4.26) A stove or roomheater set within a chimney recess – the recess should be large enough to provide room for fuel hod, ashbin and tools. A soot door in the soffit may be needed to clean the flue unless the chimney can be swept through the appliance.

Fireplace storage

Fireside fuel

Do not forget that the fire needs refuelling and that some of the fuel is best stored near the fire. Decide first how the fuel will be carried in from outside, whether in log baskets, coal scuttles or hods and then decide whether these are to be visible.

If they are to be on show, then make sure that the hearth is big enough to accommodate them, otherwise plan a cupboard for them on one side of the fireplace. Woodburning fireplaces can have shelves or pockets built alongside as part of the fireplace design – but make sure that these are large, as fires consume wood far more rapidly than the equivalent volume of coal or smokeless fuels.

Accessories

There is a whole industry of ironfounders and brassfounders making fireplace accessories which range from the standard poker, tongs, shovel and brush through to bellows, trivets, pot hangers, chestnut roasters, pivot grills, firelighters, fireguards and sparkguards. The fire irons need a place to hang and the sparkguard needs a place to go when it is not standing in front of the fire. A cupboard on one side of the fireplace is not only useful for fuel, as mentioned above, but will store some of the accessories and stop them cluttering up the hearth and spoiling the appearance of the fire, especially in summer when the fire is not in use.

Chapter 5

FIREPLACE CONSTRUCTION

Fireplace recesses

Where a fireplace is built to enclose either an open fire or a closed appliance, the walls must be built in incombustible materials to certain minimum thicknesses. All fireplaces, whether against a wall or freestanding, must have a hearth. Fig. 5.1 illustrates the individual components of a typical fireplace. For the Building Regulations for fireplace recesses and hearths see pages 132–40.

Fireplace openings

Constructional lintels

It is always advisable to make the structural opening to the fireplace larger than that strictly needed for an inset fire. In the case of new houses it may not be known which type of appliance the householder will choose and, even if a small inset fire is to be installed, it makes sense to construct a larger opening which may then allow for a larger roomheater or convector fire to be installed at a later date without costly structural alterations. The SFAS recommends that this structural opening often known as the builder's opening or appliance recess should be a minimum of 800 mm (2 ft 7½ in) wide, 1 m (3 ft 4 in) high × 340 mm (1 ft 1½ in) deep. Most freestanding room heaters, wood-burning stoves and convector fires can be accommodated within these dimensions. Tall workshop stoves would need a higher opening unless they stand in front of the chimney breast (Fig. 5.2).

Arches

The top opening to a fireplace serving an open fire or freestanding appliance can also be a masonry arch. It should be designed with a sufficient curve to be self-supporting. The

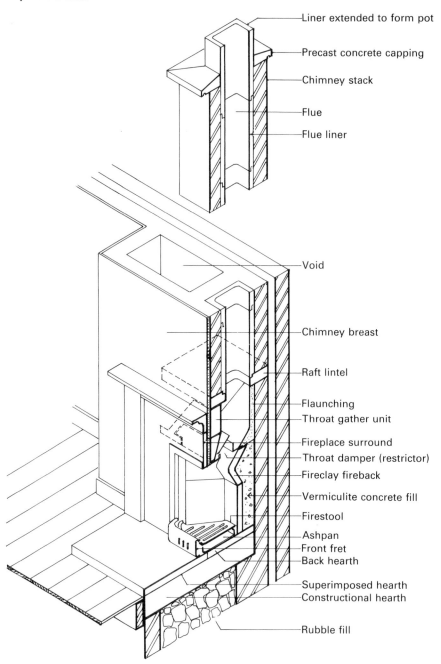

Liner extended to form pot

Precast concrete capping

Chimney stack

Flue

Flue liner

Void

Chimney breast

Raft lintel

Flaunching

Throat gather unit

Fireplace surround

Throat damper (restrictor)

Fireclay fireback

Vermiculite concrete fill

Firestool

Ashpan

Front fret

Back hearth

Superimposed hearth

Constructional hearth

Rubble fill

5.1 Fireplace anatomy.

use of steel arch bars is not to be recommended, as they will corrode in time with water vapour given off by the fire.

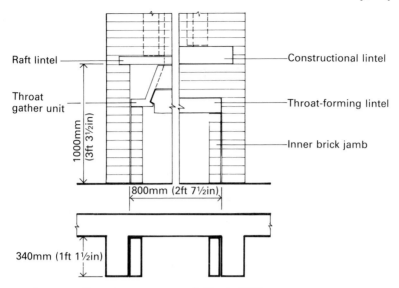

5.2   Fireplace recess dimensions as recommended by the SFAS.

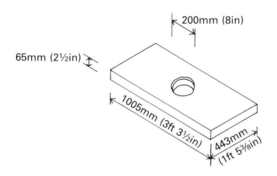

5.3   Raft lintel.

Raft lintels

Instead of using a conventional lintel, a more recent innovation is the use of the *raft lintel* (Fig. 5.3). This is a 65 mm (2⅝ in) reinforced precast concrete slab with a central 200 mm (8 in) diameter hole, which is built into the masonry and supports both the flue liner and chimney masonry above. Where this is used in conjunction with a roomheater or box stove, the flue pipe from the top of the appliance can connect directly into the raft lintel opening. Where it is used for an open fire, then a precast concrete throat unit, as described below, can be placed underneath, supported on additional brick jambs either side of the fireplace.

Register plates

Where a roomheater or stove is to be installed in a fireplace recess, the traditional way of closing the fire is to use a *register plate*. To comply with CP 131:1974 it should be not less than 1 mm thick and are normally constructed of 1.5 mm galvanised sheet steel. It should be well supported and sealed with fire cement on all four sides. It can be let into the brickwork at the back and sides or be screwed to metal angles. An appropriate sized hole should be made for the appliance flue and a well-fitting access door made for sweeping the chimney.

Throats

The walls of the fireplace have to be gathered in to form a shape like a truncated pyramid to join the firebox to the flue. The point where this shape meets the flue is called the throat. Good throat formation is essential for the fireplace to operate properly. The narrowing of the flue at this point increases the initial velocity of the smoke into the flue and prevents smoke spilling into the room. At the same time the throat reduces the amount of air filtering through the room and therefore stops unnecessary heat being wasted up the chimney. If a throat is constructed in corbelled brickwork the opening should be 100 mm (4 in) front to back and about 300 mm (12 in) wide.

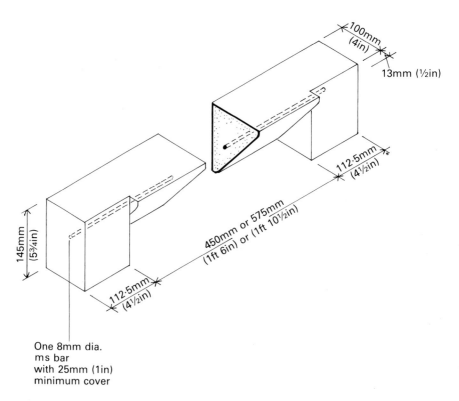

5.4   Throat-forming lintel to BS 1251:1970, viewed from inside fireplace.

Throat forming lintels

One method of forming the throat is to use a *throat-forming lintel*. This should conform to BS 1251:1970 and is inserted under the constructional lintel at the height required to suit the particular fireplace. It is made of reinforced precast concrete with a sloping inner face to provide a smooth passage for the smoke and air to pass up the flue (Fig. 5.4).

Throat units

An alternative to using a throat forming lintel is to use a proprietary precast concrete *throat unit* or *throat gather*. These are recommended by the SFAS as they simplify the gathering of the fireplace opening to the flue. They incorporate a removable front brick for access to make the necessary flue connections and can be combined with various different sizes of square and round flues (Fig. 5.5).

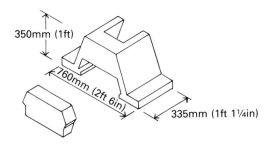

350mm (1ft)

760mm (2ft 6in)

335mm (1ft 1¼in)

5.5   Throat gather unit with removable centre-front to ease fixing of flue connections.

Throat restrictors

A *throat restrictor* is a metal damper, adjusted by a lever to regulate the size of the opening from closed to fully open positions (Fig. 5.6). BS 3376:1961 recommends that they should be fitted to all small appliances with a fire opening of less than 840 cm^2 (130 in^2).

They have two advantages: when the fire is not in use they close the flue against excessive heat loss and, when in use, can be adjusted to allow the fire to burn with the minimum air flow possible, thus ensuring that more of the heat enters the room rather than the chimney. This flexibility can also be useful with varying wind conditions.

They can also be useful in curing old smoky fireplaces which have too large a throat. By restricting the throat size, they increase the air speed through the fireplace, ensuring that the smoke is carried up into the flue rather than into the room. The restrictor should be fully open when lighting the fire and the chimney is cold and adjusted only when the fire is going well and the chimney has had time to warm up.

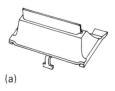

(a)

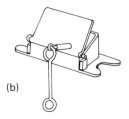

(b)

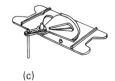

(c)

5.6 Throat restrictors
   (a) 'Rayburn Heat Saver' (by Glynwed Appliances)
   (b) two-action box damper and frame (by Dudley)
   (c) quadrant-type damper and frame (by Dudley).

Appliance chests

An alternative to building a chimney recess is to use a prefabricated *appliance chest* or *chamber* (Fig. 5.7). These are made of precast concrete components forming a box suitable for housing most proprietary open fires and roomheaters.

Coupled with a factory-made insulated chimney they are a quick and relatively cheap solution to providing a fireplace in an existing house that has no chimney.

They are also quick to erect and so are sometimes preferred by builders for installing in new houses. Some types eliminate wet trades as they are dry assembled, others are designed to be bedded in mortar or fire cement. They must all be bedded onto a constructional hearth which must be properly supported or have suitable foundations.

There are two types of chest: those with a flat slab suitable for connecting to roomheaters, and those with a hood with an internal gather for use over open fires. They are made of lightweight aggregate concrete, which gives good insulation and can easily be drilled for boiler pipe connections. They can be positioned on internal or external walls. The chests can be finished in a variety of finishes such as tiles or plaster and can incorporate any fire surround.

In order to comply with Building Regulation L22 (2) and BS 4543:1976, where a prefabricated chimney is connected to an appliance chest and is enclosed in a duct, which would be the case in most domestic situations, the casing may be made with timber studding and plasterboard, providing the timber is kept a minimum of 50 mm (2 in) away from the outer case of the chimney. Also a full height access panel must be made for periodic inspection of the chimney. This is usually positioned at the side, with access needed for any pipes and pumps connected with back boiler installations.

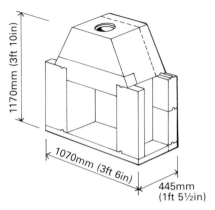

5.7 Appliance chest ('Parkachest' by Park Sectional). Prefabricated in lightweight concrete, available with or without back.

Smoke chambers

Many old fireplaces have a smoke chamber and smoke shelf built above the throat. Count Rumford advised that a smoke chamber at least as wide as the front fireplace opening and the depth of the throat plus that of the shelf 100–150 mm (4–6 in) should be constructed above the throat and slowly gathered up to connect to the flue.

The idea behind this chamber was to allow any cold downdraughts to have a space to mix with the warm up-currents from the fire, before being drawn up again out of the flue. However, Rumford was dealing primarily with very large chimneys, which would have had a good draught. In the early 1950s the Fuel Research Station proved that such a chamber was not only unnecessary but in some cases, as in short flue lengths, would impede the velocity of the flue gases and possibly cause the fireplace to smoke.

The introduction of mandatory flue liners which improve the insulation of the chimney also means that cold downdraughts are less likely and now the practice is to connect the fireplace opening to the flue at the throat, without any intermediate smoke chamber.

Chapter 6

FLUE DESIGN

Siting of flues

Placing fireplaces on internal walls has the advantage that external temperatures will have no adverse effect on the draught of the flue and the flue will take less time to heat up and cool down. Also, heat taken up by the masonry surrounding the flue will transmit itself to adjoining rooms. Chimneys in party walls of terrace houses are therefore preferable to those placed on the end walls. Centrally placed chimney stacks also allow for back-to-back flues or side-to-back arrangements, making it possible to provide fireplaces in more adjoining rooms than, say, a stack at one end of the house. Such a stack also provides good ventilation to the rooms, reducing the risk of condensation.

There are however some advantages in having the chimney on the outside wall, if serving a fireplace at ground level. It is possible to install a deep ashpit accessible from outside which allows ash to be carried directly to the dustbin and not through the house. Also, where roomheaters or stoves are connected to the chimney at ground level, it is possible to have a soot door for cleaning the flue positioned outside, which avoids all the mess associated with sweeping chimneys from inside. It is also easier to provide an underfloor fresh air inlet to a ground floor fireplace if it is placed on an outside wall.

Ventilation from flues

Open fireplace flues have the advantage of providing ventilation to the house and preventing a stuffy atmosphere by allowing fresh air into the room, thus reducing the risk of condensation, especially in houses of modern construction where improved insulation and draughtproofing of doors and windows has largely eliminated natural draughts.

Updraughts

Updraught results from the difference in pressure between the lighter column of hot gases in the flue and the colder air outside. This quite small difference in pressure within the flue creates the pull. The warmer and taller the flue the better the pull and the lower the risk of condensation within the flue.

Draught is adversely affected by:

wind blowing down chimneys;
too sharp bends in flue;
too rough a surface within the flue;
obstructions – fallen mortar, dead birds, excessive soot etc;
insufficient insulation;
air and moisture leaking in old and badly constructed flues;
open windows on the lee side of the house
(see Fig. 8.2 on p. 81).

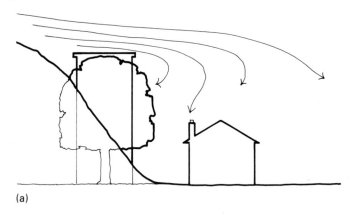

(a)

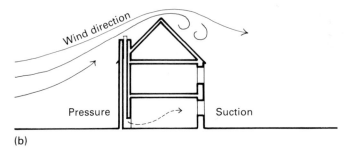

(b)

6.1 Causes of downdraughts
(a) nearby hills, trees and buildings may cause downdraughts
(b) if a low chimney stack is in a pressure zone, the suction at the face of the fireplace may cause loss of updraught.

Downdraughts

Downdraughts may be created if a chimney is lower than a nearby object on the windward side of the roof. There may also be suction on the leeward side of the house, which could cause the pressure at the bottom of the flue to be less than that at the top, thus pulling air down the flue. This usually only occurs when the wind is in a certain direction (Fig. 6.1).

In order to avoid this problem the chimney should rise above the region of high pressure, which is relatively easy if it is a neighbouring pitched roof or dormer window, but impossible if high pressure is caused by an adjacent tall building or hill. In these situations, fitting an appropriate cowl will sometimes cure the problem.

Condensation in flues

All kinds of fuel give off water vapour. Fuels with relatively high hydrogen content produce most water vapour. So long as water remains as vapour until it leaves the flue, there are no problems, but if flue gases are cooled sufficiently, condensation will occur

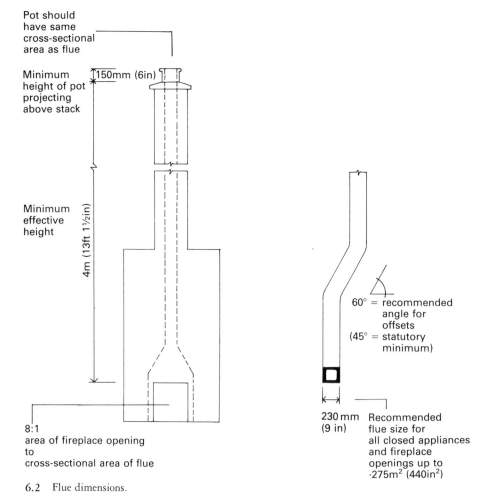

6.2 Flue dimensions.

6.3　Old flue waiting for a new house (*Jeremy Dixon*).

on the surfaces of the flue. This moisture can then combine with sulphur compounds in the flue gases and also leach sulphates from the brickwork, forming weak acids which in time will attack mortar joints, resulting in staining on upper floor chimney breasts.

Condensation can also be the result of too large a cross-section of flue, or burning excessive amounts of wet fuel or refuse.

Modern flue liners deal effectively with condensation, so this problem is only likely to occur in flues older than 1966, before the current Building Regulations demanding proper flue linings were in force.

Condensation should not be confused with damp caused by rain penetrating inadequately pointed masonry, faulty flashings or inadequate damp-proof courses in the chimney stack.

Shape of flues

The most effective flue is built straight over the fire or appliance, has no offsets and is finished with a straight sided pot. Where offsets are required these should ideally be built at an angle no less than 60° from the horizontal and should never be less than 45° to comply with the Building Regulations. The inside of the flue should have a smooth uniform bore and be clear of mortar droppings (Fig. 6.2).

Size of flues

The recommended minimum internal dimensions for a flue connected to a fireplace recess is 185 mm (7½ in) square or 200 mm (8 in) diameter. At present only 225 mm (9 in) flue liners are manufactured and this size is recommended for all closed appliances and open fires with fireplace openings up to 500 × 550 mm (20 × 22 in).

For larger fireplace openings, a general rule is that the area of the fireplace opening should be in a ratio of 8:1 of the cross-sectional area of the flue. This ratio may be reduced to 6:1 when using basket grates with a flue less than 5 m (16 ft 6 in) high.

Height of flues

The higher the flue, the better the potential draught. The SFAS advises that for a chimney to be effective it should not be less than 4 m (13 ft) measured from the top of the appliance or fireplace opening to the top of the stack. The chimney should project well above the roof and any adjacent openings, as set out in the Building Regulations. These regulations are to ensure that the products of combustion are taken well clear of the building and are also designed to prevent the chimney being positioned in an area of low pressure or suction which might cause downdraughts. The height of a chimney, when projected above a roof, should not be more than four and a half times its smallest plan dimension, unless adequately supported.

Chapter 7

FLUE CONSTRUCTION

Chimney stacks

Chimney stacks may be built of brick, block or reinforced concrete, but to comply with the Building Regulations the flue must be lined with an appropriate liner.

Alternatively there are whole flue systems which incorporate both structure and lining. The masonry chimney stack is more economical if built when the whole house is constructed. The prefabricated flues are more economical for installing in existing buildings, or new timber or steel frame buildings, when there is little or no other masonry. They are simple to erect and often do not need a skilled bricklayer to install, so tend to be cheaper in labour costs. Materials for flues and chimneys should comply with CP 131:1974.

Chimney flashings and damp-proof courses

It is important that proper flashings are provided where the chimney emerges through the roof (Fig. 7.1).

Weatherproofing the chimney stack above roof level can be achieved by inserting a dpc into the brickwork joint, level with the lowest flashing joint (Fig. 7.2).

On steeply pitched roofs this dpc is ideally stepped with the flashings up the side of the stack. An alternative is to insert a lead or copper dpc tray below the roof intersection.

However, it should be noted that any continuous dpc or tray will weaken the stability of the stack so, where for structural reasons it is undesirable to have such a dpc, the stack can be made weatherproof either by rendering or by changing to impervious bricks set in waterproof mortar. These last two solutions are advisable, in any case, where the chimney is set in a severely exposed position.

Flue construction

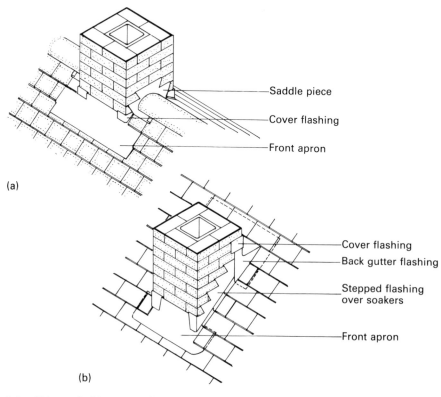

Saddle piece

Cover flashing

Front apron

(a)

Cover flashing

Back gutter flashing

Stepped flashing over soakers

Front apron

(b)

7.1 Chimney flashings in no 4 Lead
    (a) chimney stack at ridge.   (b) chimney stack in sloping roof.

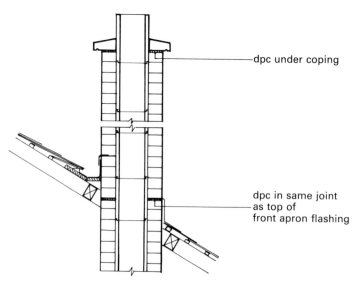

dpc under coping

dpc in same joint as top of front apron flashing

7.2 Damp-proof courses in chimneys.

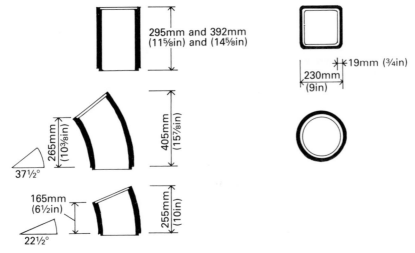

7.3 Flue liners
    Typical square and round rebated and socketed clay liners.

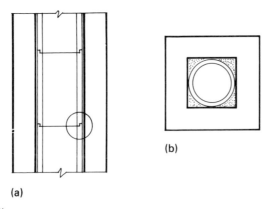

(a)

(b)

7.4 Fixing flue liners
    (a) flue liner fixed with socket uppermost to prevent condensation from flue seeping into stack
    (b) voids between round liners and square stack should be filled with vermiculite concrete.

Flue linings

Chimneys built in bricks, blocks or stone must be lined (Fig. 7.3).

Flue liners are installed prior to chimney construction so that they can be carefully bedded and left smooth inside. The sockets must be placed uppermost to allow condensation to run down inside the flue and not seep out between the lining and the masonry (Fig. 7.4). It is important that joints are smoothly pointed with cement mortar and well formed to prevent air leaks.

Square flue liners are easier to build into masonry and their shape allows the corners to fill with soot, keeping the centre cleaner for longer periods than round flues.

Round flue liners must have the voids between them and the surrounding masonry filled with mortar or lightweight concrete.

Flexible stainless steel liners dropped in from the top of the chimney stack are designed specifically for gas-fired appliances and are not suitable for fireplaces, as the gauge of the steel is too thin to resist the sulphur content of solid fuel. Also the corrugated surface of the flue liner would soon trap soot and tar deposits.

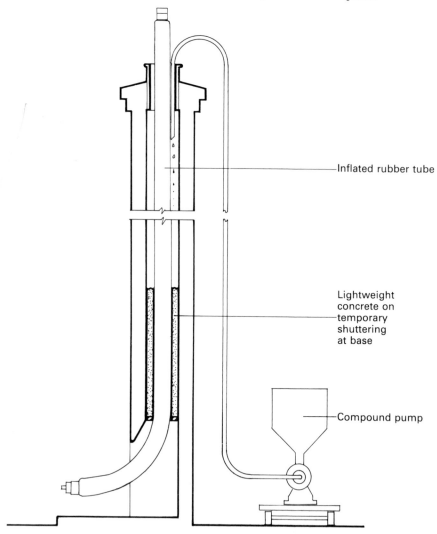

Inflated rubber tube

Lightweight concrete on temporary shuttering at base

Compound pump

7.5   Relining an existing flue; proprietary system (by Supaflu).

Lining existing flues

Lining existing flues with rigid jointed liners can prove to be both difficult and expensive requiring the cutting away of masonry to give access to joints. However, some large, absolutely vertical flues can be lined with modern liners. The liners are lowered from the top of the flue and the space between the liner and the masonry filled with a weak mix of 6:1 vermiculite concrete. One method of lining old leaking masonry flues is to use a proprietary method. A pneumatic rubber tube is inserted down the cleaned flue and centred in the flue by means of metal spacers attached to it where bends occur. The bottom of the flue is sealed off with a metal plate and the tube is inflated to the desirable diameter. A lightweight concrete (perlite or vermiculite) is pumped between the tube and the stack and allowed to set for 6–12 hours. The tube is then deflated and withdrawn and the top of the chimney walls are finished with the cement. The whole operation takes about two days for an average domestic chimney (Fig. 7.5).

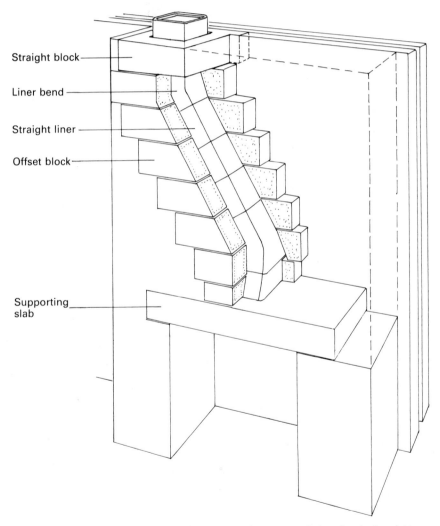

Straight block

Liner bend

Straight liner

Offset block

Supporting slab

7.6   Precast concrete chimney blocks (by Taylor and Portway), designed to be keyed into 75 mm (3 in) or 100 mm (4 in) blockwork.

Precast block chimneys

The alternative to building a masonry chimney and lining it with an approved liner is to use a precast cellular or solid concrete block (Fig. 7.6). Some makes are suitable for open fires and solid fuel appliances. They have separate or integral liners to conform to the Building Regulations and, providing they are tied in at floor and ceiling level with metal ties, can rise to a height of 13 m (43 ft). The walls of the cellular blocks have air pockets to provide maximum insulation, the pockets being laid face down. Various finishes such as cement wash or rendering can be applied. Where the chimney is built externally or emerges from the roof, it should be finished with cement rendering for weatherproofing and to maintain the insulating properties of the flue. Similarly the stack may be brick clad when emerging from the roof, a suitable corbelling block being made for this purpose.

Another advantage is that it is possible for two men to erect a 7 m (23 ft) flue of this type in a few hours, as against several days for a conventional brick flue. This is because there are fewer mortar joints to be hardened off.

Prefabricated insulated chimneys

A prefabricated insulated chimney is sometimes a convenient alternative to a masonry flue, particularly for installing a fireplace where no chimney exists, or for timber or light framed buildings where masonry would be inappropriate. It can be situated inside or outside the building and should comply with BS 4543:1976. The steel walls of the flue are lined with insulation material and some have stainless steel inner linings, others have refractory liners (Fig. 7.7). Both types provide a fully-insulated flue, ensuring even temperature throughout the length of the flue. They take up less space than masonry or concrete block flues, are quick to erect, and flues with stainless steel outer casings look good enough to be left uncovered or decorated.

Insulated chimneys with stainless steel liners have, however, only a likely length of life of about 20 years, unlike the chimneys with refractory liners which should last the lifetime of the building. They also require very regular cleaning to ensure that the inner lining does not corrode (Fig. 7.8).

The chimney systems consist of a complete kit of parts including chimney lengths, tees, elbows, terminals, firestop spacers for where they pass through floors and roofs, dust stops, insulation sleeves, roof flashings, storm collars, roof and wall supports and inspection doors. Internal flue diameters range from 100 to 250 mm (4 to 10 in). They must not be supported on the appliance, but on a concrete raft lintel or be suspended from the floor joists with a plate.

The sections are lightweight, easy to install, some joining together with a twist action of positive mechanical seal, thus eliminating wet trade work (Fig. 7.9).

The Building Regulations part L22 (see pages 150–1) should be referred to for the positioning of joints in relation to structure, angle of offsets, distances of combustible materials from the flue, access for inspection and the location of the flue within buildings.

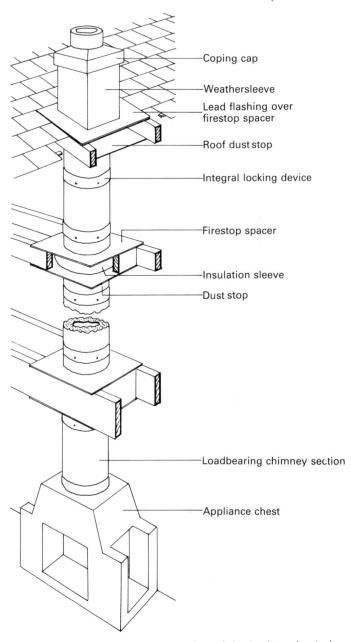

Coping cap

Weathersleeve

Lead flashing over firestop spacer

Roof dust stop

Integral locking device

Firestop spacer

Insulation sleeve

Dust stop

Loadbearing chimney section

Appliance chest

7.7   Prefabricated insulated chimney, ('Parkaflue' by Park Sectional) – galvanised steel outer casing, mineral wool insulation and ceramic inner lining.

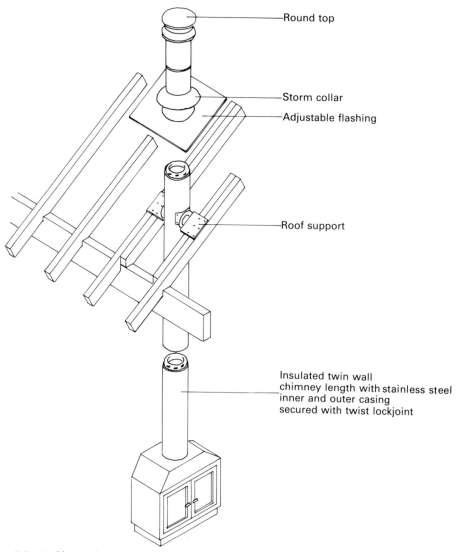

Round top

Storm collar
Adjustable flashing

Roof support

Insulated twin wall
chimney length with stainless steel
inner and outer casing
secured with twist lockjoint

7.8   Prefabricated stainless steel flue (SM system by Selkirk Metalbestos) — suitable for open
fires and stoves with all fuels up to 540 °C (1000 °F).

Flue pipes

Flue pipes are pipes which connect appliances to the chimney flue. They should not be
confused with flue liners or flue blocks.

Flue pipes serving solid fuel appliances and open fires may be constructed of cast iron
or mild steel. Heavy quality asbestos may only be used above the first 1.8 m (6 ft). For
minimum thickness of flue pipe materials and the proximity of combustible materials,
see the Building Regulations L8 and L9 (pages 145–8).

7.9   Two men erecting a Selkirk Metalbestos stainless steel flue (*Selkirk Metalbestos*).

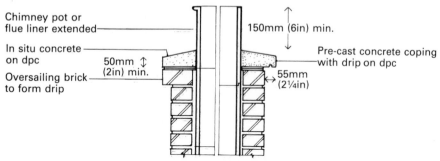

7.10   Chimney cappings.

Chimney cappings

Traditionally, brick chimneys are finished with a slightly oversailing course of bricks which provides a drip to stop the rain from running down the sides of the stack. This brick course is finished with flaunching, a sloping cement fillet to throw the rain off and to seal the joint between the stack and the chimney pot.

Nowadays it is considered better to finish the oversailing brick course with insitu concrete laid on top of a damp proof course (dpc) with the top weathered to the outside edge which should have a minimum thickness of 55 mm (2¼ in) (Fig. 7.10).

Alternatively a simply precast concrete capping can be bedded on a dpc directly onto the main stack without the need for a projecting brick course. The capping should have a weathered top surface to throw off the rain, project about 55 mm (2¼ in) from the chimney face and have a drip grooved into the underside.

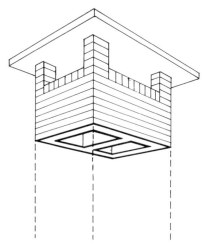

7.11   Dovecote top
Sometimes used to protect large flues from rain and downdraughts.

Dovecote tops

For large flue openings which need protection from the rain, a dovecote top is sometimes built in place of a chimney pot. This is a flat precast concrete slab supported on bricks or concrete at the corners which shields the flue from direct rain and downdraughts, whilst allowing the smoke to escape in all directions.

A dovecote top may also be suitable for a situation where downdraughts are caused by winds.

The concrete slab should be weathered to throw off the rain, and the liner should project slightly from the stack (Fig. 7.11).

Chimney pots

The purpose of a chimney pot is to lead the smoke clear of the brickwork and to protect the flue exit from swirling air currents caused by the chimney stack itself.

Where there is a cluster of pots in the same stack, avoid finishing all the pots at the same level, as this can cause syphonage, allowing smoke to pass from one flue to another. Raising the level of one pot is usually sufficient to break this effect.

Chimney pots should not be too tall otherwise the flue gases, having left the warm insulated flue, may cool down too quickly, and the updraught will be slowed.

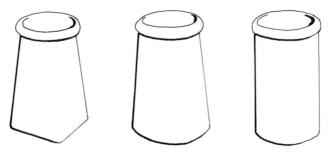

7.12   Chimney pots
       Typical shapes to suit square and round flue liners.

Pots are made in burnt clay and can be obtained in terracotta, red, buff or blue-black, so that the colour of the pot can be chosen to suit the predominant colours of the surrounding brick, stone or slate.

Today, instead of using a conventional chimney pot, it is more usual to extend the flue liner a minimum of 150 mm (6 in) above the flue capping. This ensures the smoothest passage for smoke to leave the chimney – particularly important for the open fire.

Old unlined flues, however, will be fitted with chimney pots. Ideally these should have the same cross-sectional area as the flue and should not be unduly constricted at the top. In practice they tend to be round pots sitting on square flues. The abrupt change from square to round can sometimes cause downdraughts. It is better therefore to fit a chimney pot with a square base which can either continue as a square section or taper gradually to a round cylinder (Fig. 7.12).

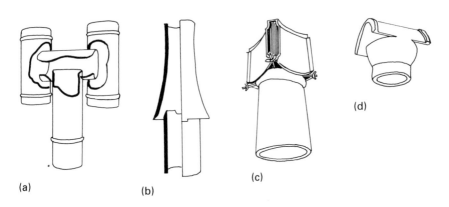

(a)   (b)   (c)   (d)

7.13   Terminals and cowls
       (a) steel or earthenware anti-downdraught cowl (by OH Ltd)
       (b) 'Marcone' anti-downdraught clay terminal (by Red Bank)
       (c) galvanised metal chimney cowl (by Colt)
       (d) clay bonnet for capping disused flues, yet allowing for ventilation (by Red Bank).

Terminals and cowls

Open fires are best fitted with a straight-sided pot with the same area and preferably the same shape as the flue. However, in some situations the chimney may be adversely affected by downdraughts caused by nearby buildings, hills, trees or freak wind conditions.

In these cases the fitting of an anti-downdraught terminal or cowl may be effective. There are various designs. Some incorporate a 'venturi' principle and others an ejector action which converts a downdraught into an updraught irrespective of strength or direction of the wind. The SFAS however is somewhat sceptical about the benefits of cowls, saying that 90% of flues should not need them as there is usually enough ventilation from the room to create sufficient updraught.

The SFAS points out that cowls are unlikely to help overcome downdraught due to a high pressure zone extending over a chimney terminal as a result of neighbouring tall structures or trees. They are more likely to be of some use in preventing downdraughts from downward wind currents (Fig. 7.13).

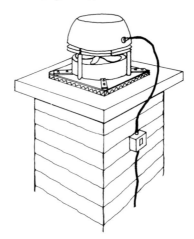

7.14 Chimney fan
'Exhausto' electric fan (by Strax), mounted on glass fibre anti-vibration mat to chimney capping.

Chimney fans

If a flue is properly constructed and has the right cross-sectional area to suit both the height of the flue and the size of the fireplace opening, and the throat is properly designed, then the fire should draw well without smoking.

However, there may be instances where it is not possible to get all the factors right. A typical instance is where a large fireplace opening is fitted to an existing flue with too small an area. Here it would be impossible to rebuild the flue without tearing the whole house apart. In this situation it might be worth thinking about a chimney fan (Fig. 7.14).

The fan sits directly on top of the flue, resting on a vibration mat and fixed into the flue with steel brackets. The fan is made of cast aluminium to resist corrosion and should run all the time the fire is lit. It is connected to an adjustable speed control which is mounted near the fireplace so that the fan speed can be easily regulated. The fan can also act as a ventilator in summer, when the fire is not in use.

The big disadvantage to installing such a fan is that in order to sweep the flue the fan must be removed. As the sweep's brushes are pushed up the flue, so the bristles are pushed back and it is impossible to bring the brush down again, without the brush fully emerging from the top of the flue, so that the bristles can reverse. This means that access onto the roof for dismantling and refixing the fan must be easy, both for sweeping the chimney and servicing the fan. So it would not be advisable to fit such a fan to a tall chimney in a ridge position. A more suitable application would be a relatively short flue, protruding from a flat roof accessible from the house by a roof hatch.

Spark arresters

Chimneys in thatched roofs or in closely-wooded areas are sometimes fitted with spark arresters. In fact, insurance companies sometimes demand that one is fitted before agreeing to insure a thatched house.

The problem with spark arresters is that they should have a mesh of not less than 6 mm ($\frac{1}{4}$ in) square to be truly effective. The fineness of this mesh means it soon becomes clogged with soot and tar and then blocks the flue, so it is very important to fix a spark arrester in a place where it can be easily and frequently cleaned.

The mesh can be of stainless steel or copper, fixed into a frame and is either fitted above the chimney pot, so allowing the flue to be swept, or at the bottom of the flue, where it must be easy to remove for sweeping the flue.

Spark arresters are made to measure to suit particular conditions and are generally undertaken by the local blacksmith.

Sparks from fires are usually only from those which burn timber or coal. A smokeless fuel is less likely to create sparks.

Chapter 8

CHIMNEY MAINTENANCE

Sweeping chimneys

For chimneys to function properly, they must be swept regularly. For grates burning only smokeless fuels, once a year is probably sufficient. For coal-burning fires, the flue will need sweeping two or three times during the heating season, as coal produces a lot of soot. Traditionally the chimney was swept in September, at Christmas and just before spring cleaning. For fires which have back boilers and are therefore used most of the year round, the chimney may have to be swept more frequently.

Wood fires, particularly those burning a lot of wet wood, will build up tar which is not easily dislodged by a brush, but sweeping at least twice a year is advisable to ensure that any loose flaking or partially-burnt cinders are removed. There is a nice story of an ancestral home which had a flue that was so badly filled with layers of tar that the chimney no longer drew properly. The factor was called in to deal with the problem and his remedy was to fire a shotgun up the flue which successfully cracked the tar lining and brought it all clattering down. Not a solution, however, one would necessarily recommend for small domestic flues.

For roomheaters burning smokeless fuel, the flue need only be swept once a year, but the throat within the appliance should be brushed at least once a month. Chimneys are still swept with a brush, with horizontal bristles quite a bit wider than the flue. The brush is inserted up the chimney with short lengths of bamboo, cane or polypropylene rods which are screwed together with brass connecting pieces. As the brush is pushed up the flue so more rods are added. The sweep pushes the brush up with a rotating action, to ensure that all particles are removed and that the rods should not come undone. As the brush emerges from the pot so the bristles are reversed, enabling the brush to be brought down again in the manner that it went up.

At the fireplace opening, the sweep will place a canvas-covered frame with two openings, one for inserting the brush and the other for attaching a vacuum cleaner which sucks up the dirt as it is dislodged. This makes the whole operation far cleaner than in the old days when the whole room had to be covered in dust sheets.

Vacuum cleaning of flues by itself will remove most of the soot, but is not enough to dislodge tar deposits or more serious blockages, which must still be removed by sweeping with rod and brushes.

Blockages in chimneys can be removed by lowering a coring ball down the chimney.

Any soot doors into the flue should be positioned with the underside not less than 600 mm (2 ft) above the floor, to enable the sweep to insert the rods. Before fitting any terminals or cowls, make sure that they are of sufficient diameter for the sweep's brush to emerge.

Sweeps are not necessarily easy to find. Ask the local approved coal merchant or look in the yellow pages of the telephone directory.

Smoke test

In order to test a flue for airtightness, a smoke test is applied in the following way. Two people are needed, one at the top of the flue and one at the bottom to light an oil rag, smoke pellet or smoke cannister in the flue. The man at the top holds a plastic bag over the pot and the man at the bottom plugs the flue with a sack filled with straw. Smoke will then be seen to emerge from any leaks in the masonry.

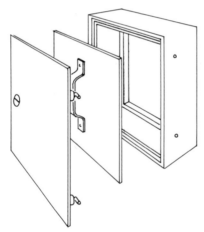

8.1 Soot door
     Cast-iron frame and outer door secured by turnbuckle and sheet steel inner door, (by Dudley).

Soot doors

Soot doors may be needed for access to sweep chimneys, where it is not possible to sweep the chimney through the appliance or where it would be inconvenient to remove, say, a freestanding stove, breaking any seals in the process in order to gain access to the flue.

Soot doors may also be needed for access to bends or offsets within the flues.

Soot doors should comply with BS 1294:1946 and are generally made in cast iron with mild steel and brass fittings. The finish can be fine cast, galvanised or, for internal use only, vitreous enamelled.

	W	H
	(mm)	(in)
The standard nominal sizes are:	150 × 225	(6 × 9)
	225 × 225	(9 × 9)
	225 × 300	(9 × 12)
	450 × 450	(18 × 18)
	450 × 600	(18 × 24)

A soot door is made up of an inner sheet steel door and an outer cast iron door – both doors should operate easily and give a reasonably airtight fit when closed. (Fig. 8.1)

Smoking fireplaces – causes and remedies (Fig. 8.2)

Blockages

The most obvious cause of a smoking fireplace is an obstruction in the flue. This might be a bird's nest, excessive soot, mortar droppings in the bottom of offset bends or protruding mortar joints from flue liners. The sweep's brush should remove light materials, and a scraper fixed to the rods may be able to dislodge protruding mortar joints. Another method is to lower a metal coring ball, the diameter of which should be 25 mm (1 in) less than the size of the flue.

Badly-formed throat

Many old fireplaces will have a badly-formed throat or even no throat at all. Sometimes the throat may also lead to a large smoke chamber, which will reduce the speed of the gases moving up the flue. This should be remedied by improving the shape of the throat with bricks bedded in lime mortar and finished with a smooth lime mortar rendering so that the fireplace gathers up to a rectangular throat approximately 300 mm (12 in) wide × 100 mm (4 in) deep. While this is being done, it is also very worthwhile to fix a throat restrictor so that the opening can be adjusted to suit the needs of the fire – fully open when lighting up and partially closed when the fire is burning well.

Fireplace opening too high

If the fireplace opening is more than 550 mm (22 in) above the grate, then the smoke is more likely to trickle back into the room. The opening can be reduced by fixing a hood or a glass or metal plate to reduce the opening height. It should not be lowered too much, otherwise insufficient heat will come into the room.

Wrong size of flue

Too big a flue for a fireplace may cause smoke, as it never really gets warm enough to

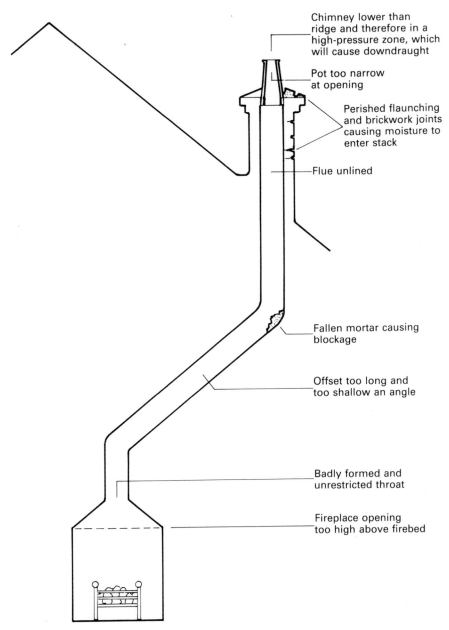

Chimney lower than ridge and therefore in a high-pressure zone, which will cause downdraught

Pot too narrow at opening

Perished flaunching and brickwork joints causing moisture to enter stack

Flue unlined

Fallen mortar causing blockage

Offset too long and too shallow an angle

Badly formed and unrestricted throat

Fireplace opening too high above firebed

8.2 Chimney faults.

draw well. Putting in a flue liner or pumping lightweight concrete round an inflatable rubber tube (see page 68) will reduce the flue size. With too small a flue for the size of open fireplace, nothing can be done except to rebuild the flue or to fix a fan to the top of the chimney (see p. 76). An alternative is to install a roomheater or convector fire.

These appliances reduce the air flow and maintain a higher temperature in the flue gases and so do not require such a big area of flue as an open fire.

Air starvation

Open fires must have an air supply to burn well. This is not often likely to be a problem but it is just possible that with an extremely well draughtproofed house with solid or carpeted floors and a fireplace with an unrestricted throat, not enough air will be getting into the room to replace that being drawn up the chimney. The remedy is to fix floor grilles near the hearth in suspended timber floors and, for solid floors, either remove draughtproofing round doors or fix a high-level grille in or over the door.

Steady downdraught

Where there is a steady downdraught, this may be caused by the chimney top being in a high pressure area, causing suction at the bottom of the flue, thus drawing smoke into the room. This may also occur with short chimneys in single-storey houses or top-floor flats where the suction through doors and windows may overcome the natural pull of the chimney (see Fig 6.1).

Raising chimneys above the region of high pressure may overcome this but they should be built to the Building Regulation requirements for height and structural stability – otherwise keep doors and windows within the room closed and see that they are draughtproofed.

Draught-inducing cowls may help to create a stronger updraught, but are less likely to be of use than preventing downdraughts from downward wind currents.

Intermittent downdraught

Downward striking winds often occur where chimneys are near higher buildings or are on the lee slope of a hill or in the bottom of a valley.

To prevent this, fix a draught-inducing cowl or finish the flue with a 'dovecote' top (see Figs. 7.11 and 7.13).

Badly-built offset

If the flue has an offset which is too long, inclines at too shallow an angle or is positioned too soon above the fireplace throat, the flue is unlikely to draw well. The only remedy is to open up that part of the flue and try to improve the offset – but this in itself may not be possible, as presumably the reason it was offset in the first place was to avoid some other fireplace or flue overhead. It might be possible therefore to divert part of the flue into an adjacent flue more directly over the fireplace. This assumes that such a flue is no longer used for a fireplace or any other function, such as providing permanent ventilation to the room or acting as a duct for an extract fan.

Air leaks

Flues must be airtight. If there are leaks the ingress of cold air will cool the flue gases and reduce the draught. This can be caused by faults in the brick joints or external rendering, or by a break in a 'withe', the wall between adjacent flues. These faults can be detected by a smoke test – brickwork joints should be repointed and rendering repaired. Flue pipes from appliances should also fit snugly into the flue and these joints should be made with soft asbestos rope, string or tape and top dressed with fire cement.

Unsuitable chimney pot

A small round chimney pot sitting on a large square flue will restrict the flue outlet opening and might cause the smoke to back down the flue. Ideally the pot is straight sided and the same size and shape as the flue. Square based pots which taper gradually to a smaller round diameter at the top will provide a much smoother passage for the flue gases, which will begin to slow as they cool off towards the top of the chimney.

Chapter 9

FIREPLACE APPLIANCES

Choosing an appliance

There are a vast number of fireplaces on the market. The basic decision is whether to have an open fire or some form of stove or roomheater. The big advantage of roomheaters is that they are far more efficient than open fires, both in the running costs and heat output, but nevertheless they do not have the attraction of the open fire. Although many incorporate glass panels through which the fire can be seen, they still are not quite as attractive as the roaring blaze of a good open fire. There are, of course, compromises – some open fires can be fitted with back boilers, which will heat a few radiators and hot water, which can dramatically increase the overall efficiency of the fire from as little as 30 per cent to as much as 65 or 70 per cent depending on the appliance. Other designs incorporate double skins so that convected air can be added to the room as well as the radiant heat from the flames. See pages 86–112 for detailed information about the types available and pages 155–61 for the names of manufacturers.

Choosing the correct size of fire for the size of room is important. Table 9.1, prepared by the SFAS, of maximum room sizes and heat outputs for various appliances, gives a guide for initial selection.

Heat Outputs

Open fires with high-output back boilers, spaceheating and hot water

For preliminary selection of an appliance the following minimum figures can be used. Where an adjustable throat restrictor is incorporated in an open fire, the size of the room may be increased by 7 m³ (250 ft³).

Roomheating for an open fire	0.05 kW/m³	(5 Btu/h ft³)
Domestic hot water supply	1.2 kW	(4000 Btu/h)
Radiator and pipework transmission	0.5 kW/m²	(160 Btu/h ft²)

Table 9.1 Maximum Room Sizes for Open Fires

Nominal fire size	Open fires	Open fires with boilers	Open fires with boiler and adjustable throats
350 mm (14 in) bedrooms and small rooms only	28 m³ (1000 ft³)		
400 mm (16 in)	50 m³ (1750 ft³)	42 m³ (1500 ft³)	50 m³ (1750 ft³)
450 mm (18 in)	57 m³ (2000 ft³)	50 m³ (1750 ft³)	57 m³ (2000 ft³)

Roomheaters

When selecting a roomheater, choose an appliance with an output capacity of not less than the following figures. Outputs are based on doors being closed. Precise values vary appreciably, according to the insulation and exposure of the room and personal preferences. If the roomheater output is larger than the room it needs to supply then it will burn less fuel and need refilling less frequently.

For rooms of approx 28 m³ (1000 ft³) 0.07 kW/m³ (7 Btu/h ft³)
For rooms of approx 57 m³ (2000 ft³) 0.06 kW/m³ (6 Btu/h ft³)
For rooms of approx 85 m³ (3000 ft³) 0.05 kW/m³ (5 Btu/h ft³)

Convector open fires

Depending on the size of the appliance, these are usually suitable for rooms up to 64 m³ or 85 m³ (2250 or 3000 ft³).

Manufactured fireplaces

A fireplace manufacturer can mean two things: one who makes the *appliance* or one who makes the *surround*. Sometimes a manufacturer will provide both, and sometimes a surround manufacturer will supply a surround to suit the appliance chosen. All fireplaces, including the simplest open hearth to burn logs, are called appliances and are classified in the Building Regulations as *Class I Appliances*.

An *Approved Fire* means an appliance which has been tested to British Standard requirements and approved by the Domestic Solid Fuel Appliances Approval Scheme. This is an independent body which reports to the National Coal Board. The list of approved appliances is published annually by the Solid Fuel Advisory Service jointly with the Solid Smokeless Fuels Federation. Note that this list will not include woodburning appliances unless they are also designed to burn solid fuels. Also it will not include many reproduction stoves, foreign fireplaces and some modern designs for which there are not yet test standards. So the fact that an appliance is not labelled 'Approved' does not necessarily mean that it is not effective.

So the first thing to decide is what sort of fireplace should be installed. Set out below are descriptions of the different types available which can be broadly classified as Inset Open Fires, Freestanding Open Fires, Roomheaters and Stoves.

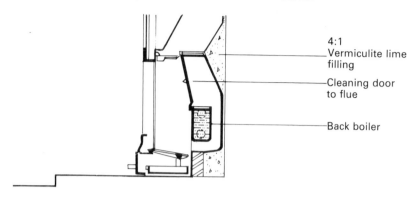

4:1
Vermiculite lime filling

Cleaning door to flue

Back boiler

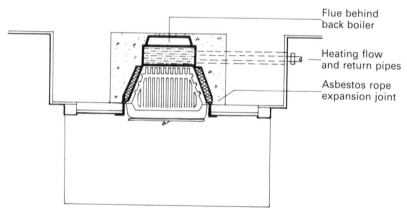

Flue behind back boiler

Heating flow and return pipes

Asbestos rope expansion joint

9.1   Typical inset open fire with back boiler.

Inset open fires

This type of fire is set into a chimney breast recess, normally with splayed sides, and comes in nominal 400 and 450 mm (16 and 18 in) widths. A smaller width of 350 mm (14 in) and larger widths of 500, 550 and 600 mm (20, 22 and 24 in) are also available but are much less common (Figs. 9.1 and 9.2).

These fireplaces are made up of firebrick back and sides, a grate and an ashpan. Some have air inlet controls with an adjustable knob in the ashpan front, or the ashpan front can be left open for air control. Some include a *throat restrictor* or *damper* to control the amount of draught up the flue, operated by a lever at the top of the fireplace. This is highly desirable if maximum efficiency and good control of the fire are to be achieved. If

9.2 'Lexham' inset open fire (by Glynwed Appliances), with stainless steel front and angle trim (*Glynwed Appliance Ltd*).

such a damper is included, then it should be easily removable by the sweep for cleaning the flue. Optional extras normally include a *deepening bar* or *overnight burning plate* which is fitted above the fire front or *fret*, to allow more fuel to be piled on at night. Most fires claim to burn for 10 hours unattended with these plates in position.

These fires are often described as overnight burning or continuous burning, which means the same thing. Some inset fires have a *drop front*, a solid flap which drops forward horizontally to reveal more of the open fire shielded behind bars. This will give out more radiant heat and be more pleasing to look at. Most inset fires can be fitted with gas burners for easy ignition. If gas is not available in the house, then a gas poker attached to a small gas cylinder or an electrically operated flame torch make convenient alternatives.

Inset open fires with back boilers

Most inset fires can be fitted with *back boilers*, often supplied by the same manufacturer. In fact in a house without central heating, where the open fire will be used most of the time during the winter, it makes sense to trap this heat source for further provision of hot water or space heating or both. The running costs will not be all that much more than running a simple open fire, except that it must be remembered that the radiators will only be kept hot so long as the fire is kept stoked, which may mean keeping the fire in during the night as well. Back boilers are often described as boiler flue sets and the manufacturer will advise which makes of fireplace they are designed to fit (Fig. 9.3).

There are two types of back boiler: A smaller model with outputs of about 3 kW for providing hot water to a cylinder, usually 114–136 litres (25–30 gallons) plus one small radiator or towel rail for the bathroom. Larger models up to 6.6 kW are known as 'high-output back boilers' which are designed to give domestic hot water plus serve four to five radiators, or more if there is some other provision for the hot water supply.

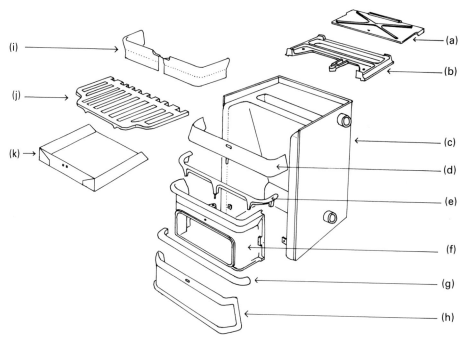

(i)
(j)
(k)
(a)
(b)
(c)
(d)
(e)
(f)
(g)
(h)

9.3 Parts of an inset open fire with a back boiler
('Parkray 29' by T. I. Parkray)

(a) boiler damper blade
(b) boiler damper platform
(c) boiler
(d) overnight burning plate
(e) deepening bar
(f) inner front

(g) decorative trim
(h) ashpan cover
(i) firebricks
(j) bottom grate
(k) ashpan

Back boilers are made from cast iron or mild steel. Back boilers which serve radiators should only be connected to an indirect cylinder, which preferably should not be further than 4.6 m (15 ft) away from the boiler.

Back boilers which provide domestic hot water only and where an indirect cylinder is not installed, should be glass lined in soft water areas to avoid corrosion. In hard water areas, they should have a removable plate to permit descaling the inside of the boiler.

Back boilers have manual control dampers to adjust the hot water output and temperature.

Inset open fires with underfloor draught

Another method of being able to burn the denser solid fuels is the inclusion of an underfloor draught. In solid ground floor construction the air inlet will have to be constructed with pipes laid in the concrete and carried to the outside air. It is advisable to have two ducts, preferably from two directions, coming to a balancing chamber from

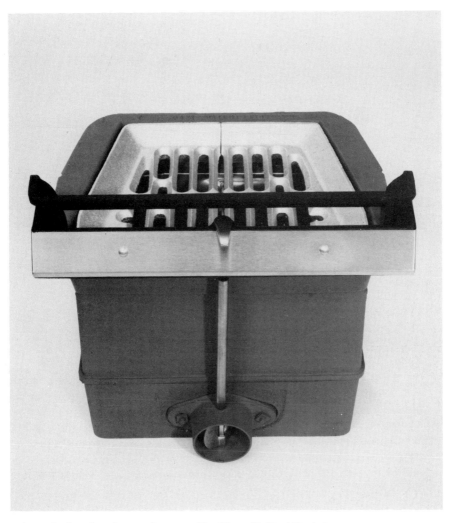

9.4   Underfloor draught open fire grate, ('Baxi Burnall') (*Baxi Heating*).

which a short length of pipe can connect to the fireplace air vent. This is to prevent the possibility of suction, created by a negative pressure on one side of the house, causing the fire to smoke. In suspended timber floors with adequate all-round ventilation through sleeper walls and unblocked airbricks, the provision of ducts should not be necessary. On floors above ground, it may be more difficult to fit air ducts within the thickness of the floor, particularly in existing houses. Air ducts should not connect to cavities in cavity wall construction (Fig. 9.4).

Underfloor draught fires are usually fitted with deep ashpits which generally only need emptying twice a week. Ashpits can be removed in three ways:

1. A simple lift-out ashbox which lifts out from under the fire grate.

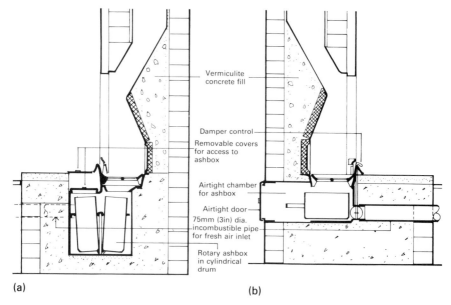

Vermiculite concrete fill

Damper control

Removable covers for access to ashbox

Airtight chamber for ashbox

Airtight door

75mm (3in) dia. incombustible pipe for fresh air inlet

Rotary ashbox in cylindrical drum

(a)   (b)

9.5   Underfloor draught open fires (by Baxi)
      (a) inset open fire with underfloor air inlet and rotary ashboxes
      (b) inset open fire with underfloor air inlet and ashbox accessible from outside.

2. An outside ashbox can be fitted where the fire is placed on a ground floor outside wall, complete with an airtight door – ashes can then be taken direct to the dustbin without being carried through the house.
3. A rotary ashbox which is suitable for overnight burning fires, where it would be inconvenient to put out the fire in order to remove the ash. These have two semi-circular ashboxes, which can be rotated so that the empty one is placed under the fire and the full one can be lifted out from a plate in the floor in front of the grate (Fig. 9.5).

Hole-in-the-wall fires

'Hole-in-the-wall' fires are underfloor draught inset fires (see above) which have been raised about 300 mm (12 in) above floor level, giving the appearance of a hole in the wall. Despite the fact that they are well above floor level, the Building Regulations still require that a constructional hearth be built into the floor. Alternatively the hearth level is often raised level with the underside of the fire opening to provide a long horizontal shelf for fireside seating or for adjacent log storage underneath. Such fires will function just as satisfactorily as an underfloor draught fire positioned at hearth level (Fig. 9.6).

The frames to finish the opening come in various finishes such as stainless steel, brass, copper or bronze; sometimes marble or small brick slips are used. The frames are generally rectangular but some 'feature' fires have circular openings and therefore more truly deserve the name hole-in-the-wall.

9.6 'Hole-in-the-wall' fireplace
(HW5 by Bell), in stainless steel or bronze finishes, with underfloor draught grate
(*A. Bell & Co. Ltd*).

9.7 Fan-Assisted fire
'Parkray Fan Fire' (by T. I. Parkray). A two-speed electrical fan is concealed in one or
other of the hobs. Bronze lustre finish (*T. I. Parkray*).

Fan-assisted inset open fires

In order to have a better draught and to be able to burn the denser manufactured fuels, some inset fires are fitted with fans. The fans are positioned in the front of the fire or may be incorporated in the surround. The fans have two speeds and need connecting to a nearby 13 A electricity supply. Fans will always make a noise and, although manufacturers claim that they are quiet in running, it may be worth checking that the noise level is acceptable before deciding to install such a fire. The fans are economical to run, using no more electricity than a 40 W bulb.

A fan-assisted open fire can be a useful alternative for situations where it is difficult to build in an underfloor air duct (Fig. 9.7).

Convector open fires

The open fire is not an efficient way of heating, as it only supplies radiant heat and much of the heat can be lost up the chimney, particularly if the throat is badly designed.

There are now, however, some appliances which combine the appearance of an open

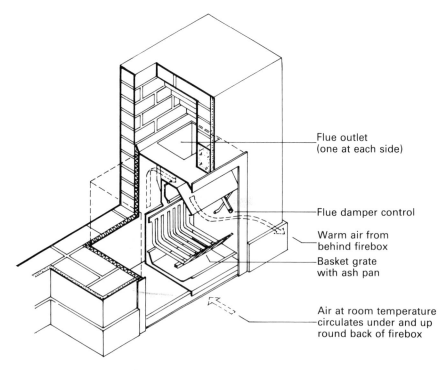

Flue outlet
(one at each side)

Flue damper control

Warm air from
behind firebox

Basket grate
with ash pan

Air at room temperature
circulates under and up
round back of firebox

9.8   Convector inset open fire
Section revealing action of convected warm air in the Jetmaster Fires.

9.9   Convector open fire
('Extra 850' by Jetmaster) – wide opening convector inset open fire, shown with optional curved steel lintel for arched openings (*Jetmaster Fires Ltd*).

fire while giving out convected heat into the room. Manufacturers claim that they can be as much as four times as efficient as a simple open fire.

Fresh air, either from the room itself, or from an underfloor duct, is directed in at the base of the appliance and passes into a chamber behind the firebox, from which warm air is directed back through either insulated ducts to adjacent rooms or grilles at the side or top of the chimney breast. In inset convector open fires, the warm air from behind the firebox comes out through an opening within the top of the appliance. The smoke from the open fire is taken to the flue via two openings which bypass the convected air. This type of convector open fire can be installed in existing fireplaces without the necessity of disturbing the surround or making holes in the chimney breast for hot air grilles. (Figs. 9.8 and 9.9).

Some types have doors and are effectively stoves designed to be built into a fireplace recess, often just using the space around the back and sides of the appliance to produce convected heat. Appliances with doors have the advantage of making the fire easier to light initially, generating more heat and enabling the fire to be kept in overnight. (Fig. 9.10).

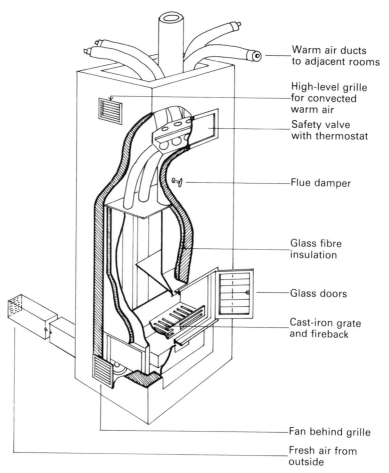

Warm air ducts
to adjacent rooms

High-level grille
for convected
warm air

Safety valve
with thermostat

Flue damper

Glass fibre
insulation

Glass doors

Cast-iron grate
and fireback

Fan behind grille

Fresh air from
outside

9.10 Open fire with ducted warm air
('Impuls air' by Keddy).

Freestanding convector open fires

Convector open fires are open fireplaces contained within metal bodies complete with canopies or hoods and are designed to give off convected heat as well as radiant heat from the open fire. They are therefore more suitable for the larger room. They are sometimes referred to as a *feature fire* and indeed some of the designs are dramatic and eye-catching. They are also sometimes referred to as *freestanding* open fires. This is somewhat of a misnomer as, depending on their design, they are not necessarily totally freestanding but very often must stand within a fireplace recess – particularly so if a back boiler is incorporated and all the attendant plumbing would need to be concealed within the fireplace. They are called freestanding to distinguish them from the 'inset' open fires which are built into the chimney breast (Fig. 9.11).

9.11 Freestanding convector open fire
('Windfire' by Keddy). Double-skinned steel plate construction with high-level warm air grilles. Multi-fuel grate with optional glass doors (*Keddy Home Improvements Ltd*).

Some models can stand in front of a chimney breast and be connected into the flue with a short length of pipe. Others are designed to be wall hung, in which case they must be very securely fixed and will still require a constructional hearth at floor level.

9.12 Freestanding open fire ('Jøtul no. 7' by Norcem). Cast-iron hearth with matt black steel smoke hood (*Norcem (UK) Ltd*).

Models which are designed to be truly freestanding in the middle of the room can be connected to a prefabricated insulated chimney, but the flue will need supporting at every second length of flue pipe, about 1.5 m (5 ft) which may be a problem where the ceiling is high or the fire is positioned in a double-height space (Fig. 9.12).

Gas fuel-effect fires

Gas fuel-effect fires are commonly known as gas log or gas coal fires. For those who wish to have some of the beauty of the open fire without the sweat of tending and refuelling, a gas log fire may be the answer (Fig. 9.13). At first glance they are deceptively real, but the illusion is not sustained for long, although there are truly real flames, the arrangement of logs and coals never changes. They are rated as Class I appliances (even though they are gas appliances) which means that all the regulations regarding hearths and flues for open fires will apply.

Gas fuel-effect fires are more expensive to run than a radiant gas fire and are much less efficient in heat output. The apparent heat may be partly due to psychological reasons.

The components are made up of a burner tray, complete with gas pipe and gas cock connections. In the tray stands a cast-iron grate, onto which silica sand and ember material is placed. Then imitation logs, coals or fir cones, made of heat refractory materials, are placed in a random arrangement (Fig. 9.14).

This arrangement can be adjusted when the fire is cold, so that an even flame pattern

9.13   Gas wood-effect fire
(Model M18 by Real Flame) giving a deceptively good illusion of a real log fire (*Real Flame*).

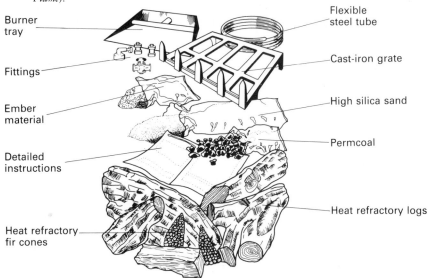

Burner
tray

Fittings

Ember
material

Detailed
instructions

Heat refractory
fir cones

Flexible
steel tube

Cast-iron grate

High silica sand

Permcoal

Heat refractory logs

9.14   Components of a gas wood-effect fire
(by Real Flame) (*Real Flame*).

is achieved. The gas is diffused through these materials and produces a yellow flame which will deposit a little soot on the logs. For this reason the flue should be swept once a year.

To make sure there is sufficient air for combustion, an airbrick within the room is recommended.

As with all open fires, fireguards should be fixed to protect children and the elderly.

These fires can be connected to natural gas and some models can be operated on liquefied petroleum gas (LPG). Other models can be operated with propane bottled gas, in which case the gas bottle must be stored outside the house with gas supply piped inside to the fire. Some models are supplied with only an on/off gas control tap which needs a match or taper to light the fire. A safer and easier system is to have a pilot light, which includes a flame failure device to cut off the gas should the flame fail for any reason. Other models are fitted with spark ignition (piezo electric) which lights the pilot which in turn lights the main burner.

Gas fuel-effect fires should be installed to comply with the manufacturer's instructions and in accordance with the requirements of BS 5258:1980 Part 12.

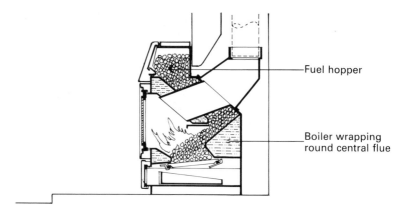

Fuel hopper

Boiler wrapping round central flue

9.15　Gravity fed roomheater
('Housemaster de luxe' by Trianco Redfyre).

Roomheaters

Roomheaters are what used to be known as slow-combustion stoves. A rather curious new name, it seems, because anything that heats a room, whether it is an open or enclosed fire, is a roomheater. But the term has come to mean a modern enclosed stove, usually for burning solid fuels. Appliances burning only wood, however, are still generally called stoves, which adds to the confusion. Similarly, workshop or studio stoves could easily well be described as roomheaters as they are closed stoves which will burn all types of fuel. The next section on wood burning stoves gives a complete picture of all the closed appliances available.

Many roomheaters have glass doors through which the fire can be viewed but which are not normally opened except for lighting and refuelling the fire.

Some models are gravity fed, which means that they have top opening lids through which fuel is fed into a hopper and gradually let down into the firebed. These types have the advantage of generally staying in for 24 hours before needing refuelling (Fig. 9.15). Roomheaters come in various sizes with ratings from 3 to 13 kW (10 000 to 45 000 Btu/h).

Roomheaters generally have controls on the front to adjust the amount of draught. Some rely on a damper in the flue and others can control the draught thermostatically.

Most roomheaters are designed to burn smokeless fuels, but a few models can burn house coal and are known as 'smoke eaters'. They are equipped with a primary air inlet at the top of the firebox. The fuel is made to burn downwards and the products of combustion are burnt as they pass through the firebed, consuming its own smoke and thus conforming with the requirements of the Clean Air Acts, and can therefore be used in Smoke Control Areas.

9.16   Recessed roomheater
('Esse Elite' by Smith and Wellstood). Small neat roomheater with high output back boiler. Copper lustre finish (*Smith and Wellstood Ltd*).

Roomheater types

There are basically two types – those designed to be partially recessed into a chimney breast recess which are sometimes called stand-in roomheaters and those which are freestanding (Figs. 9.16 and 9.17). Most models can be fitted with back boilers for hot water and space heating.

9.17 Freestanding roomheater ('Parkray GF' by T. I. Parkray). Sizes range from 6 to 13.6 kW. Chocolate brown lustre finish (*T. I. Parkray*).

Fixing roomheaters (Fig. 9.18)

Some recessed roomheaters can be fitted into a standard fireclay fireback and use the existing throat as a flueway. Others will need a short length of pipe to protrude into the flue. If an existing recess is too large then the space round about the recessed roomheater can be used as a convection chamber by fixing a non-combustible panel with adjustable grilles to close the gap between the heater and the edge of the fireplace recess – this type of installation is sometimes referred to as the *free-inset* method.

If this space is not used as a convection chamber then the space round the sides of the recessed roomheater should be filled with vermiculite concrete to act as insulation.

Freestanding models can be fitted in front of the chimney breast with flue pipes connecting to the flue from the back or top of the appliance. They can also sit inside a fireplace recess with the flue pipe connecting to the flue through a metal register plate or concrete raft lintel. They can also be completely freestanding within a room and be connected to a prefabricated insulated chimney. If this sort of situation is envisaged, then the flue will need supporting at 1.5 m (5 ft) intervals, which can be a problem if the roomheater is positioned centrally with a high ceiling.

Most roomheaters allow for the flue to be swept through the appliance. Where this is not possible, the heater will have to be removed and flue connector pipes disconnected and subsequently resealed. Alternatively soot doors should be provided. For the heater placed on a ground floor outside wall, the soot door can be fixed outside. Alternatively a soot door placed in the flue above the stove can be masked by a picture.

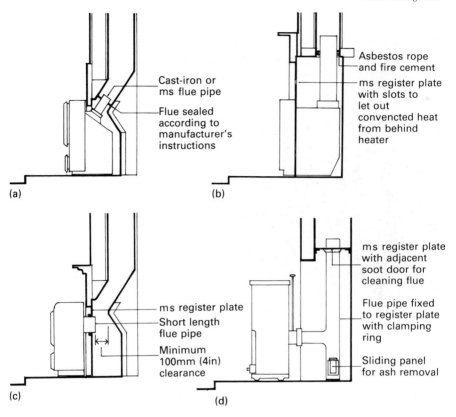

Cast-iron or
ms flue pipe

Flue sealed
according to
manufacturer's
instructions

Asbestos rope
and fire cement

ms register plate
with slots to
let out
convencted heat
from behind
heater

(a)

(b)

ms register plate
Short length
flue pipe

Minimum
100mm (4in)
clearance

ms register plate
with adjacent
soot door for
cleaning flue

Flue pipe fixed
to register plate
with clamping
ring

Sliding panel
for ash removal

(c)

(d)

9.18   Fixing roomheaters and stoves
    (a) recessed roomheater built into an existing fireplace
    (b) 'free-inset' method of installing a room heater
    (c) freestanding roomheater fixed to vertical register plate
    (d) freestanding stove fixed to flue with horizontal register plate.

For efficient working and safety from noxious fumes all joints between heaters and flue pipes must be tightly sealed – with soft asbestos rope and fire cement.

Wood-burning stoves

There are a large number of wood-burning stoves on the market, some modern designs and others reproductions of traditional models (Fig. 9.19). Many of them are imported from Scandinavia and Northern Europe where, unlike Britain with its plentiful supply of cheap coal, the tradition of burning wood in stoves has continued almost uninterrupted (Fig. 9.20).

Construction

Wood-burning stoves are generally made of cast iron or steel plate. The thicker the

9.19 'Poppy' stove (by Hunter)
Cast-iron solid-fuel stove 10 kW, with a
choice of 'poppy' or 'iris' design
enamelled tiles. Large bow-fronted
glazed door (*Hunter and Sons (Mells) Ltd*).

metal the more robust and satisfactory the stove. Most have a matt black finish which is easy to keep clean, using graphite cream polish, whereas others have vitreous enamelled finishes in a variety of colours.

A few makes have tiled surfaces to the top or sides (Fig. 9.21). Some can have an alternative finish of copper lustre or vitreous enamel (Fig. 9.22). One or two stoves are also made in terracotta with iron doors. Stoves must have well-fitting moving parts and airtightness of joints is essential – a point to be especially noted when buying second-hand or reconditioned stoves. Some models come in sections which will need to be fitted together with asbestos rope and fire cement.

Flue pipes for stoves

The stoves can be connected to existing flues with short lengths of fluepipe coming off the top or the back of the stove. Where there is no chimney they can be connected to a prefabricated insulated flue. (See Fig. 9.18 for fixing roomheaters). Generally speaking the more the stove projects into the room, the more convected heat will be given off.

Air control

Most stoves have primary and secondary air inlets adjusted by controls on the front of the stove. Some require dampers in the flue to control the burning rate and a few have

9.20 Cast-iron woodburning stove
('Jøtul 201 Turbo' by Norcem). Closed stove with secondary combustion chamber
claiming 70% efficiency (*Norcem (UK) Ltd*).

9.21 Tiled stove
('Godin Belle Epoque' by Ellis Sykes).
Multi-fuel stove shown with the original
'art nouveau' 1903 tiles – these tiles can
be interchanged with any other 152 mm
(6 in) wide tiles (*Godin SA*).

thermostatically-controlled dampers. Some stoves employ the Franklin principle of incorporating a baffle plate, which forces the air in the stove to move in an 'S' shape to ensure the even and complete burning of logs.

The bigger the firebox the longer the log length, which means less time spent preparing the wood if one is sawing the wood oneself, as opposed to having it delivered cut to the required lengths. Split logs dry quicker, are easier to burn and to pack more tightly into the stove, leaving less air spaces and thus ensuring more efficient and continuous combustion (Fig. 9.23).

Other fuels

Wood stoves will also burn peat and some can be adapted to burn coal and smokeless fuel. As solid fuel burns at higher temperatures than wood, the body must be robust enough to withstand the greater heat, so some of the higher gauge steel and thinner cast iron stoves will need firebricks to protect the sides and all will need a grate on which to place the solid fuel, and preferably an ash tray too. These can sometimes be provided as optional extras but some models are only suitable for burning wood.

9.22 'Esse Dragon' (by Smith and Wellstood)
Victorian design in solid fuel and woodburning versions. Wood-burning model has side
door entry for logs. Scroll on top removes to reveal boiling plate. Matt black, copper and
midnight blue lustre or grey vitreous enamel finishes (*Smith and Wellstood Ltd*).

Refuelling times

Most stoves will burn continuously for from 8 to 12 hours, although a few small models
will need stoking more often, which means they will not stay in overnight. Some of the
larger models will burn for as long as 16–24 hours, useful if the stove is to stay in over a
weekend when the house is unattended.

Output ratings

Wood-burning stoves are rated from 2.5 to 20 kW (9000 to 68 000 Btu/h) though the

9.23 'Sherwood' Stove (by Spencer)
Cast-iron multi-fuel closed stove with large drop down door capable of receiving 450 mm
(18 in) long logs (*Philip Spencer Stoves Ltd*).

most common sizes are 5–12 kW (17 000–41 000 Btu/h). The size of the room will
dictate the size of the stove and the manufacturer will advise on appropriate sizes. Not
only is it important to have a stove large enough to heat the room adequately but it is
also important not to install too big a stove where the room might become intolerably
hot and also visually overpower a small room by sheer size. The quoted output ratings
can only be approximate as performance will depend upon the type and dryness of the
fuel, and output will be lower if the doors are open or the dampers are regulated for slow
overnight burning.

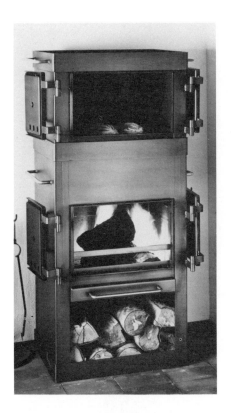

9.24 Wood burning convector stove ('Scan no. 11' by Petal Agencies). 8–30 kW with baking oven on top. Optional coal burning grate. Similar models available with fan to improve heat distribution (*H. Krog Iversen and Co.*).

9.25 'Godin Oval' stove (by Ellis Sykes). Cast-iron multi-fuel stove of 1888 design with steel outer casing in brown, dark green or grey enamel finishes (*Godin SA*).

9.26 Box Stove
('Magnette' single door wood-burning stove by Quebb). Heavy-duty plate steel construction with cooking hotplate. Optional side shelves and back boiler. Can be converted for solid fuel (*Quebb Stoves*).

Weight

Stoves can be very heavy; they vary in weight from small sizes around 75 kg (165 lb) to monsters of 400 kg (880 lb). If a very heavy stove is to be placed on a constructional hearth within a suspended floor, then care should be taken to ensure the concrete is adequately reinforced and well supported at the edges.

Wood-burning stove types

There are wood-burning stoves to suit every type of decor. As well as the many beautiful 'Scandinavian' style stoves (Fig. 9.24), there are many Victorian designs which have been reproduced (Fig. 9.25). There are three main types of wood-burning stove:

9.27 Open Stove
('International' by Trianco Redfyre). Multifuel stove with back boiler 13.2 kW. Glass door slides up and over to reveal open fire. Lever converts slotted coal grate to closed wood burning grate (*Trianco Redfyre Ltd*).

1. Box stove This is essentially a freestanding box-shaped stove with small metal or glass doors which are kept shut except for lighting and refuelling. Some incorporate a hotplate for cooking on top (Fig. 9.26).

2. Open stove with doors These are generally larger boxes which have glass or metal doors which can be opened to give the appearance of an open fire, but have the advantage of being able to close the doors to allow the fire to stay in overnight or when there is no one in the house (Figs. 9.27 and 9.28).

9.28 Reproduction Franklin stove
('Franklin Giant' by Bell). Large-capacity wood-burning stove with swing out barbecue grille (*A. Bell & Co. Ltd*).

The more efficient types have convector hoods or outer casings which allow additional heat to be convected into the room. Glass doors will quickly become discoloured with tar from burning wood but this can be cleaned off with damp wire wool.

3. Workshop or studio stove These are generally tall cylindrical or rectangular closed stoves, so called because they were often used for economical heating of large work-shops, but the smaller sizes are equally suitable for domestic use. They will generally burn a variety of fuels including timber, coal and smokeless fuels as well as combustible waste materials (Figs. 9.29 and 9.30).

9.29 'Studio' stove (by Trianco Redfyre). The original elegant 'Pither' Victorian stove. Highly efficient, convector anthracite-burning stove with self-feeding hopper and close-burning damper. Cast-iron body with black stove enamel or stainless steel outer casing (*Trianco Redfyre Ltd*).

In addition to these three main types of wood-burning stoves there are also wood-burning cookers, central heating boilers and central heating multi-burners which have a large capacity and output 17–140 kW (60 000–480 000 Btu/h) and will burn any combustible waste material, straw bales or rolled newspaper as well as conventional fuels.

Optional extras

Some wood-burning stoves can be fitted with back boilers and some of the open stoves can be fitted with a grille plate or rotisserie. Some models can be fitted with an electric fan for forced convection and ducts can be connected in order to heat adjacent rooms. Sparkguards, steel mesh curtains for open stoves, tongs and pokers are other useful accessories.

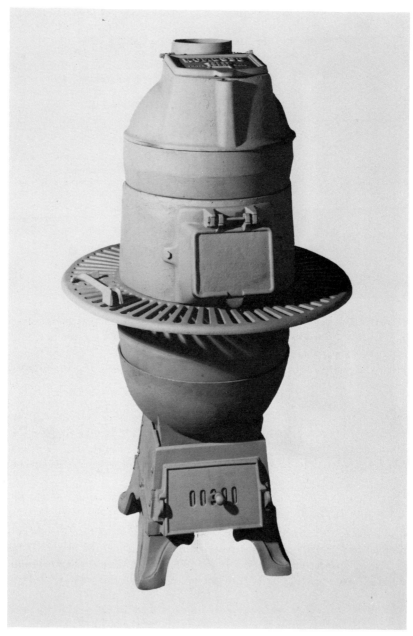

9.30　Workshop stove
('Esse Romesse' by Smith and Wellstood). Solid fuel and refuse-burning stove in various sizes. Constructed in cast-iron sections fitted together without screws or cement. No firebacks. Gallery or 'tutu' is an optional extra (*Smith and Wellstood Ltd*).

Chapter 10

FIREPLACE SURROUNDS AND ACCESSORIES

Fireplace surrounds

The fireplace surround is a decorative surface surrounding the fireplace opening. Many manufacturers claim to sell fireplaces when in fact all they are selling is the surround. The fireplace is literally the place where the fire burns.

Designs for surrounds abound – many are hideous and while some are reasonable reproductions of medieval or neo-classic styles, most modern designs leave a lot to be desired.

A surround is not essential. Many modern fireplaces are designed simply as holes in walls of fairfaced brickwork or stone (Fig. 10.1). Others in plastered walls may be finished with nothing more than a stainless steel frame – but surrounds do serve one useful purpose in providing a surface which should be easy to clean, if the fire should smoke.

There are no mandatory building regulations regarding fireplace surrounds but certain principles should be observed in their design and they should conform to BS 1251:1970 (Fig. 10.2). They should be of incombustible materials capable of withstanding a temperature of 350 °C (660 °F) at least for an area immediately surrounding the fireplace opening. Perimeter frames and mantelshelves may be made of timber.

The concrete backing to a fireplace surround should be a minimum of 40 mm (9/16 in) thick and should be all in one piece at the back. Any tiles should be a minimum of 9.5 mm (3/8 in) thick and the surround should not be thicker than 50 mm (2 in) for at least 50 mm (2 in) round the fireplace opening to ensure good entry of air into the throat and for making gas connections. This can be increased to 55 mm (2¼ in) for those surrounds incorporating metal frames.

The surround should have a pair of fixing eyelets both sides with a 6.5 mm (¼ in) hole, one pair to be within 300 mm (12 in) from the top.

The surround must be fitted with fireguard sockets; two 9.5 mm (3/8 in) eyelets, 300 mm (12 in) above the hearth and their position should exceed the fireplace opening

10.1 Solid brass frame with glazed doors ('Rotherglow' by Victoria Stone). Kit includes steel fixing brackets and optional curtain firescreen (*Victoria Stone Ltd*).

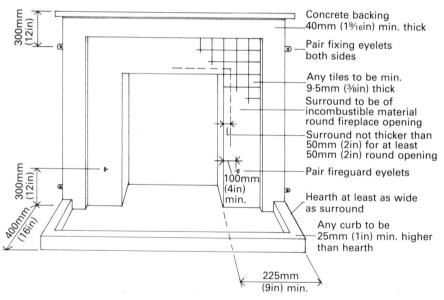

10.2 Fireplace surround design requirements as laid down in BS 1251:1970.

by a minimum of 100 mm (4 in).

If a hearth (i.e. a superimposed hearth) is supplied with the surround, the width should not be less than the surround and should be at least 450 mm (18 in) wider than the fireplace opening – the hearth should project a minimum of 400 mm (16 in) from the back of the surround. If a curb is fitted to the front and side edges of the hearth it should be at least 25 mm (1 in) higher than the top of the hearth.

Fireplace surround materials

Fireplace surrounds, whether proprietary or purpose made, can be built in many different materials which are summarised as follows. For names of suppliers see the list of manufacturers and suppliers at the end of the book.

Stone Most stone is suitable for fireplaces but the most commonly used are York, Cotswold and Derby. Portland stone can be polished to an almost marble-like appearance. Local stone can be cheaper as transport costs are reduced.

Reconstructed stone (Fig. 10.3) Reconstructed stone is available in many different colours, shapes and sizes. There are regular or random shaped blocks and slips (tiles) up to 38 mm (1½ in) thick. Reconstructed stone is cheaper than real stone and easier to lay. For those people who wish to save labour costs, DIY fireplace surround kits are available. The kits contain blocks, hearth stones, mantelshelves and pointing materials.

Slate Slate surrounds and hearths are available in the following colours: Welsh blue/black, Lakeland green and Cornish blue/brown and grey. Welsh slate, when highly polished, can look almost black and can be overpoweringly dark for use in a surround. It is however a useful material for hearths, as it can be precisely worked and is easy to keep clean.

Marble Polished marble is probably the most expensive of all materials used in fireplace surrounds, but it has a most luxurious appearance and is one of the easiest materials to keep clean of soot and ash. The colours range from white to black with reds, greens and yellows in between. It is generally imported from Italy but also comes from France, Portugal, Greece, Africa and Pakistan.

Terazzo Terazzo is a conglomerate of marble chips bonded with cement or resin and made up into prefabricated slabs. The slabs can be reinforced so that they can be made stronger than natural marble and they are also cheaper than marble, with a similar appearance but without the veins. Terazzo slabs can be made to order or bought as proprietary surrounds and hearths.

Brick Bricks have been fired to high temperatures in their manufacture and are therefore most suitable for fireplace surrounds, including the sides of fireplace recesses. For recesses with basket grates without firebacks, firebricks should be used for the back of the fire. Arches can be formed for the fireplace openings, and mantelshelves and hearths can be made up with matching brick slips.

10.3   Reconstructed stone fireplace ('Mulcheney' by Minsterstone) (*Minsterstone*).

Briquettes Briquettes are small bricks, normally available in reds and buffs. The standard size is 146 × 57 × 38 mm (5¾ × ¼ × 1⅛ in). Many special shapes can be obtained for corners, curbs and mantelshelves.

Brick tiles or slips Brick tiles, sometimes called brick slips, come in various colours and are made in thicknesses from 16 to 25 mm (⅝ to 1 in). They can give an illusion of brickwork when stuck with adhesive to a chimney breast and can easily be fixed by a layman. The face size is usually the old imperial size of real bricks 219 × 67 mm (8⅝ × 2⅝ in). Some manufacturers produce '**L**'-shaped corner tiles to cope with external corners which retain the illusion of real brickwork.

Quarry tiles are hard burnt clay tiles and come in red, heather brown, buff and blue/black colours. They are normally 152 mm (6 in) square and come in 16, 19 and 22 mm (⅝, ¾ and ⅞ in) thicknesses. Rectangular and hexagonal quarry tiles are also available. Specials include bullnosed edges and coved skirtings. The tiles can be used for hearths, even under basket grates.

10.4   Cast-iron fireplace and basket
     ('Serpentine' surround with 'Mildmay' basket by Acquisitions), in burnished cast iron or
     painted to order (*Aquisitions Fireplaces Ltd*).

Ceramic glazed tiles Ceramic glazed tiles are often used for fireplace surrounds as the high gloss finish is the easiest of all fireplace materials to keep clean. Glazed tiles come in standard sizes of 138 mm (4¼ in) and 152 mm (6 in) square and 6.5 and 9.5 mm (¼ and ⅜ in) thicknesses, the thicker tiles being preferable. Glazed tiles are not suitable for use in hearths immediately under basket grates.

Cast iron (Fig. 10.4) Many Victorian fireplaces were made of elaborately designed cast iron and some of these designs are still being reproduced today. Existing cast-iron fireplaces can be renovated by being cleaned by shot-blasting or stripped of paint and then polished. Cast iron, although immensely strong, can fracture quite easily, so great care should be taken when moving such a surround.

Wood (Fig. 10.5) As wood is a combustible material, it should be kept away from the immediate fireplace opening. This area is usually finished with tiles or marble, which are both incombustible and easier to keep clean than wood. Traditionally, oak was used for mantelpieces but, due to its expense, it has been superseded by cheaper hardwoods,

10.5 Carved pine fireplace surround ('Wendover' by Patrick Fireplaces) (*Patrick Fireplaces*).

pine and hardwood veneered blockboards. The timber selected must be kiln dried or well seasoned to avoid splitting and cracking from the heat of the fire. Wood can be varnished, stained, polished or painted to suit the surrounding decor.

Fibrous plaster (Fig. 10.6) Reproduction fireplaces are often made up of fibrous plaster with a painted finish. Moulds from intricate designs can be more cheaply reproduced than hand carved in the original materials.

Plastics Old designs can also be reproduced in glass reinforced polyester (GRP) and polyurethane foam (PU) which can be moulded to any shape with considerable accuracy. They can be sawn, drilled and fixed as easily as timber.

Firebacks

The back of the fireplace can be protected in several ways.

10.6 Fibrous plaster fireplace surround ('Seymour' by Roger Pearson) (*Roger Pearson*).

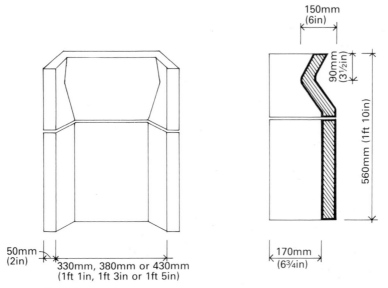

10.7 Fireclay firebacks
Typical two-piece fireback to BS 1251.

150mm
(6in)

90mm
(3½in)

560mm (1ft 10in)

170mm
(6¾in)

50mm
(2in)

330mm, 380mm or 430mm
(1ft 1in, 1ft 3in or 1ft 5in)

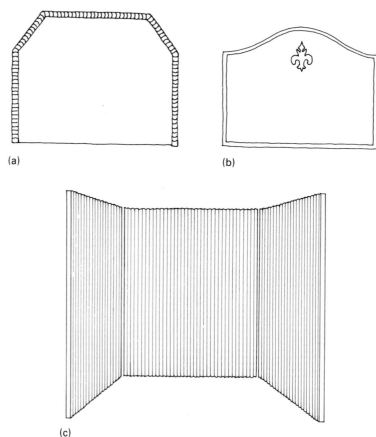

(a) (b)

(c)

10.8 Cast-iron firebacks (by Kingsworthy)
(a) rope twist (b) plain fleur-de-lis (c) reeded panels

Inset fires are fitted with *standard firebacks* (Fig. 10.7). These are made of fireclay or ciment fondu. They are made in two- or four-piece patterns suitable for the standard fireplace widths of 350, 400 and 450 mm (14, 16 and 18 in) and should conform to BS 1251:1970. Four-piece firebacks are easier to install and less likely to crack than those made in two pieces.

Where there is no inset fireplace or appliance complete with its own firebricks, then *refractory fire bricks* can be built into the masonry wall. Firebricks are made from fireclay and are reddish yellow in colour.

Masonry firebacks without firebricks can be protected with *cast-iron firebacks*. These also help to radiate heat into the room. They are available in traditional designs or can be made to suit the customer's own requirements. Designs are made by pressing objects into the sand of the casting bed before the molten iron is poured on. Traditionally they often incorporated heraldic motifs or were decorated more humbly with the blacksmith's handprint, a sword, a pair of scissors or a rope for the border. Reeded panels to

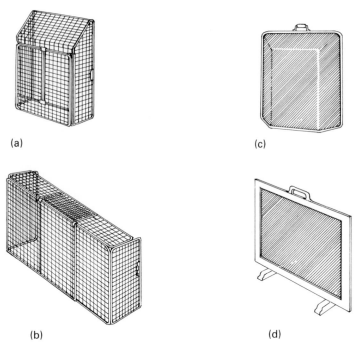

10.9 Protection from the fire
(a) BS fireguard   (b) nursery fireguard   (c) sparkguard   (d) firescreen

cover the full height of the back and sides of the fireplace recess can also be obtained (Fig. 10.8). Cast-iron firebacks are extremely heavy and need to be carefully transported. Normally they will just tilt against the masonry wall but they can also be drilled for fixing screws or lugs which should be loosely let into the wall to allow for expansion and so prevent the fireback from cracking.

Fireguards

Fireguards should be distinguished from sparkguards in that their purpose is to prevent people, particularly children, the old or infirm, from falling into an open fire and to help prevent serious burns resulting from clothing catching fire. Fireguards can be adapted for use as a sparkguard by simply adding a fine mesh screen to the guard, but as the fireguard should be in a position all the time that children or old people are around, this mesh would seriously reduce the efficiency of the fire, so it is probably better to place a separate sparkguard around the fireguard when the room is unoccupied.

Under the Children and Young Persons Amendment Act 1952, all forms of open fire whether electric, gas, oil or solid fuel must be protected with a fireguard for children under the age of twelve (seven in Scotland).

Fireguards should comply with BS 2788:1956 which recommends that the overall size should not be less than 495 mm (19½ in) high and the width should be at least 100 mm (4 in) wider than the fireplace opening. The fireguard should project at least 200 mm (8 in) from the face of the fire surround over the whole width of the fire opening and the front should be parallel with the face of the fire to a minimum height of 250 mm (10 in) above hearth level. The top of the fireguard should slope in at an angle to discourage people from using the guard to air clothes.

In order to refuel the fire, without removing the guard, the bottom of the guard should be openable to a height of not less than 125 mm (5 in). Any openable portions of the fireguard must be capable of being securely closed.

Fireguards should be securely fixed to the fire surround with two hooks engaging into eyelets to the surround 300 mm (12 in) above the hearth. These hooks should be provided with spring clips or some other suitable device so that they cannot easily be removed by small children (Fig. 10.9).

Fireguards are made of wrought iron or brass frames with mild steel mesh panels.

Nursery fireguards

The description describes a general purpose type of fireguard which can be used with a variety of larger fireplaces and appliances such as stoves and boilers, wherever the appliance is acting as an open fire and a fireguard might be necessary. These fireguards should incorporate the features described above but the overall dimensions will be bigger.

BS 3140:1967 recommends that they are not less than 600 mm (2 ft) high and 900 mm (3 ft) wide and if lower than 750 mm (2 ft 6 in) high then an openable top should be provided for the full width of the fireguard. The depth should be between 300 and 550 mm (12 and 22 in) and the front surface should be parallel to the fire over the whole width and up to a height of at least 500 mm (20 in)

Sparkguards, firescreens and fire curtains

Sparkguards

Sparkguards are normally placed in front of an open fire when a room is unoccupied, to prevent sparks flying out and possibly starting a fire. They are **not** to be confused with fireguards. In other words they are too light to prevent people from falling into the fire.

There are two types of sparkguard – freestanding sparkguard and one designed for a specific appliance.

BS 3248:1960 recommends that a sparkguard should be robust, stable and made of suitable hard and durable material. The maximum dimension of any hole in the mesh shall not be larger than 0.071 cm² (0.011 in²) and the mesh shall be securely attached to the frame, free from projecting wire ends. It should incorporate a handle sufficiently well insulated so that it can be removed without burning the hands. The guard should be 64 mm (2½ in) wider than the fire opening and not less than 470 mm (18½ in) up to a height of at least 510 mm (20¼ in) and the overall height not less than 560 mm

10.10 'Galleon SS 2251' (by Galleon Claygate).
Brass frame with folding heat-resistant glass doors and curtain firescreen set in natural stone surround (*Galleon Claygate Ltd*).

(22 in). The sparkguard should be fixed to the surround, as described above for fireguards.

Sparkguards for specific appliances should completely cover the fire opening and be capable of a firm and positive location on the appliance.

Firescreens

Firescreens are wire mesh screens which stand in front of the fire when the room is unoccupied to prevent sparks leaping out of the fire. They should not be confused with sparkguards which have sides and a top which fully enclose the fireplace opening or fireguards which have a larger mesh and are designed to prevent children from falling into the fire. Firescreens are made with forged steel or brass frames and generally have a matt black mesh often incorporating some decorative motif.

Fire curtains

Fire curtains or curtain firescreens are made of a flexible wire mesh rather like chain mail in galvanised steel, brass or copper. They are suspended from the top of the fireplace opening on curtain runners or rings and are pulled with a draw rod to the sides of the

123

10.11 Fireplace with eliptical wrought iron basket, curtain firescreen and Victorian brass fender (*Charlotte Baden-Powell*).

fire when not required. They are a neat, if expensive form of sparkguard but have the advantage over freestanding sparkguards in that they do not have to stand somewhere else when not needed (Fig. 10.10).

Fenders

Fenders came in with the arrival of coal, to contain the coal within the area of the hearth. They are normally made of perforated steel or brass, tall for narrow hearths and shorter for big hearths. Nowadays they are often replaced by a curb built of the same material as the superimposed hearth. (Fig. 10.11 and 10.12).

Canopies

Canopies or hoods have the advantage of radiating more heat into the room and also of inducing the smoke from the fire up into the chimney–a great advantage in large old open fireplaces. They are usually made-to-measure to suit a particular fireplace. Some fireplace designs incorporate such a hood as part of the appliance. They are made in copper, brass, stainless steel, aluminium, galvanised steel or black stove-enamelled

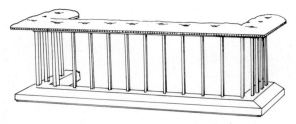

10.12   Club fender
        Constructed in brass with buttoned leather seat (by Country Style).

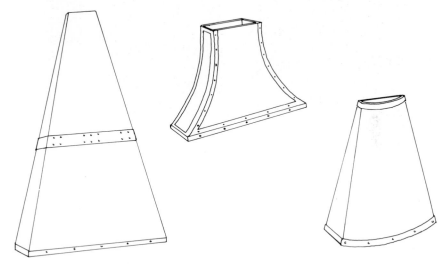

10.13   Canopies
        Made-to-measure hammered copper or stainless steel hoods (by James Smellie).

steel. In the non-ferrous metals the surface can be hammered or smooth. Hoods will get extremely hot and, in places where they might easily be touched, such as a freestanding central fireplace, should be double-skinned with an air gap or have an outer skin of some other material to act as insulation (Fig. 10.13).

Firedogs and baskets

Firedogs

Firedogs are often called *andirons*, thought to be a corruption of brandiron, endiron or the French 'landier'. They are the earliest form of fireplace equipment, today's designs being just a smaller-scale version of those found in early medieval houses. Their purpose is to lift the ends of logs off the hearth to allow the air to get underneath and to stop logs rolling out of the fireplace. They must be heavy and stable to do their job well. Early designs had hooks in front for supporting roasting spits and sometimes cup-shaped baskets on top to warm bowls of food or drink beside the fire. These are called

10.14   Elizabethan cast-iron fireback dated 1565 from Ockwells Manor, Berkshire. The men decorating the firedogs wear ionic capitals as hats (*By kind permission of Country Life*).

10.15   Contemporary mild steel basket and dogs designed by Charlotte Baden-Powell and made by local blacksmith with swinging arm at back to support kettle over fire. Flue lined, soffit inserted to close off wide chimney, the fireplace raised and a new hood lowered over the fire to improve the draught (*Charlotte Baden-Powell*).

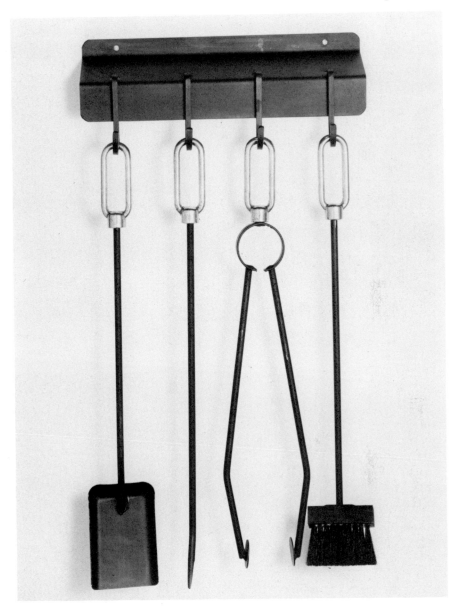

10.16 Set of fire irons
('Scan' companion set by Petal Agencies). Mild steel with brass handles (*H. Krog Iversen and Co.*).

mulling dogs. For a fireplace which burns nothing but wood, a pair of dogs is all that is needed, for the wood can be burnt directly on the hearth (Fig. 10.14). For all solid fuel however, a basket is required.

127

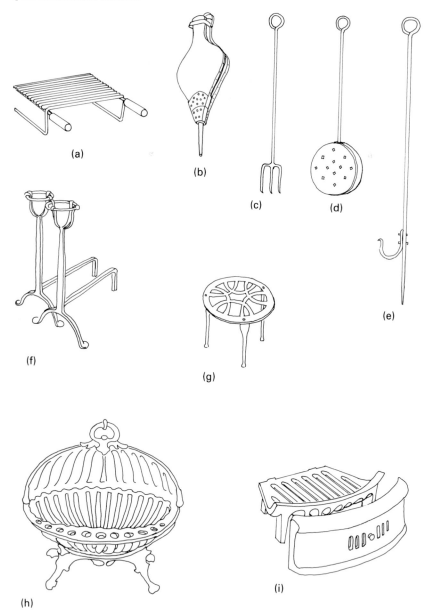

10.17 Fireplace accessories
   (a) fireplace barbecue
   (b) bellows
   (c) toasting fork
   (d) chestnut roaster
   (e) log roller

   (f) mulling dogs
   (g) brass trivet
   (h) chestnut firebasket
   (i) firestool and fret

Firebaskets

Firebaskets were introduced during the seventeenth century for burning coal. Until then, only wood, charcoal or peat was burned on open fires and a basket was needed to contain the coals. Some baskets are made with extended spikes which, as well as being suitable for coal, help to keep logs from falling out. There are many foundries making baskets, dogs and firebacks. Some are genuine copies of traditional patterns, othere are modern designs.

Many blacksmiths will make firebacks and baskets to order, and will enjoy incorporating some family motif or initials in the design (Fig. 10.15).

Fire irons

A set of fire irons consisting of poker, shovel and tongs came into use in the eighteenth century. Nowadays the set is often sold with a stand and generally incudes a hearth brush and is known as a *companion set*. Fire irons are made of steel or brass and can vary considerably in size (Fig. 10.16). A set of irons should be chosen to suit the scale of the fireplace. There are many attractive designs about, but above all they must be robust and functional. Tongs in particular can be awkward to operate and should be handled to see how easy they are to use. A *log roller* is a poker with a curved hook for rolling logs, which is a useful tool for wood fires (Fig. 10.17).

Bellows

Bellows are exceedingly useful in getting wood fires going. They were originally made from animal bladders or bellies, hence the name 'bellows', or sometimes an animal skin, where a pipe was fitted into one of the legs like a bagpipe. A flap inside the skin provided a simple non-return valve. Nowadays the best bellows are made from hardwood and leather secured with brass gimp pins.

Fireside cooking

Barbecues

The open fireplace is a good place to barbecue food, especially as British weather so often mitigates against cooking outdoors. Simple frames with cantilevered racks are available for placing amongst the coals. Alternatively charcoal containers complete with racks can be placed in the empty fireplace.

Trivets

A trivet is a small three-legged stand, usually in iron, steel or brass, to keep dishes warm by the fire.

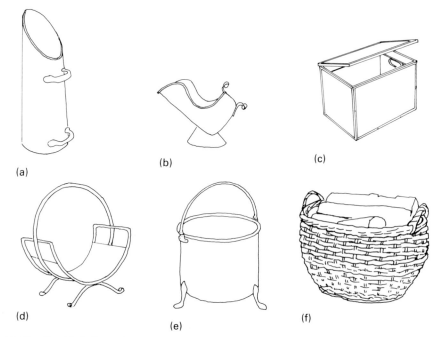

10.18 Fireside fuel containers
   (a) hard-rubber hod
   (d) wrought-iron log cradle
   (b) copper helmet coal scuttle   (c) brass fuel box
   (e) copper log bucket   (f) wicker log basket

Chestnut roasters

A chestnut roaster us a small copper or brass pan with a perforated lid for roasting chestnuts on an open fire.

Fireside fuel containers

Coal buckets and hods

Coal buckets, or scuttles as they are sometimes called, are probably easier to use if they have a lip for pouring the fuel onto the fire. These are usually made in copper or brass with a carrying handle and a handle at the back with which to tip the bucket. Coal hods may be more useful for pouring the smaller-sized fuels into stoves and roomheaters as they have a narrower mouth. There are also a variety of wooden boxes with metal liners, but these need a shovel to transfer the coal onto the fire (Fig. 10.18).

Log cradles and baskets

A log cradle is a metal basket with two open sides in which logs can be straddled and is useful for carrying fairly long logs. Otherwise logs can be carried in wicker log baskets which should not be too heavy but nevertheless be extremely sturdily made. Those with solid bottoms will last longer than those with woven bottoms.

Chapter 11

REGULATIONS AND STANDARDS

Building Regulations

The purpose of the Building Regulations concerning fireplaces is to ensure that heat-producing appliances in buildings are not dangerous to life, property or health, either directly from fire or from noxious fumes.

The Building Regulations 1976 apply to the whole of England and Wales with the exception of the Greater London Council area. A list of the regulations which are relevant to the building of fireplaces and chimneys follows.

The GLC publishes its own London Building (Constructional) By-laws in which part XII deals with flues, chimneys, hearths, ducts and chimney shafts.

Scotland has its own regulations: the Building Standards (Scotland) Regulations, in which part F refers to chimneys, flues, hearths and the installation of heat-producing appliances.

To help readers through the maze of regulations, which are not always easy to understand, the following text and illustrations attempt to summarise and provide an interpretation. They are based on the Building Regulations and only describe the London and Scottish regulations where they differ.

Readers outside the UK should apply to their local authority for relevant regulations regarding the construction of fireplaces and flues.

Building Regulations 1976 — construction of fireplaces and chimneys

D   8   Structure above foundations
D 15   Chimneys of bricks, blocks or plain concrete
E   9   Compartment walls and compartment floors
L   1   Application and interpretation of Part L
L   2   General structural requirements
L   3   Fireplace recesses for Class I appliances
L   4   Constructional hearths for Class I appliances

L	5	Walls and partitions adjoining hearths for Class I appliances
L	6	Chimneys for Class I appliances
L	7	Flue pipes for Class I appliances
L	8	Materials for the construction of flue pipes for Class I appliances
L	9	Placing and shielding of flue pipes for Class I appliances
L	10	Proximity of combustible materials for Class I appliances
L	11	Openings into flues for Class I appliances
L	12	Flues communicating with more than one room for Class I appliances
L	13	Outlets of flues for Class I appliances
M	1	Interpretation of Part M
M	2	Prevention of emission of smoke – clean air
M	4	Class I appliances

Class I appliance means a solid-fuel or oil-burning appliance having an output rating not exceeding 45 kW. It now also includes gas fuel effect fires, even though gas appliances with an input rating not exceeding 45 kW are otherwise classified as *Class II appliances*. (Appliances in excess of 45 kW are defined as *high-rating appliances*).

A *chimney* is the structure forming the flue.
A *flue* means the passage within the chimney
A *flue pipe* means a pipe forming a flue, but is not a flue liner.

Building Regulations for fireplace recesses

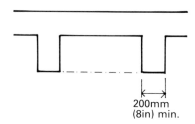

200mm
(8in) min.

11.1 L3 (2) (a and b)

L3 (2) (a and b) The back and side walls of a fireplace recess must be made of solid incombustible material.

Bricks, concrete or burnt clay blocks or in-situ concrete are considered to be incombustible materials. (In Scotland, bricks or blocks of a fire-resistant composition refer to bricks or blocks of kiln-burnt material or concrete having a density of not less than 1600 kg/m^3 or blocks of aerated concrete. These materials must be capable of withstanding a temperature of 1000 °C without significant change in their properties).

The thickness of the back and side walls to the recess must be a minimum of 200 mm (8 in). (In Scotland 300 mm (12 in), if fire-resistant bricks or blocks are not used) (Fig. 11.1).

This thickness must be carried up over the full height of the fireplace opening. (In the GLC area it must be carried 300 mm (12 in) above the fireplace opening). (In Scotland fireplace recesses must be lined with 38 mm (1½ in) fireclay unless the appliance itself is lined with 38 mm fireclay).

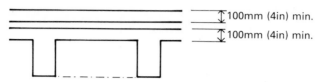

11.2   L3 (2) (b)

L3 (2) (b) Where the fireplace opening is built into an external cavity wall, then the two leaves must not be less than 100 mm (4 in) thick. (In Scotland this dimension must be increased to 150 mm (6 in) unless fire-resistant bricks or blocks are used) (Fig. 11.2).

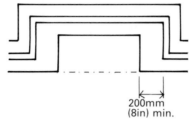

11.3   L3 (2) (a and b)

L3 (2) (a and b) Where a chimney breast projects externally and the front of the jambs (side walls) are flush with the inside wall, then the jambs, whether they be single construction or the inner leaves of a cavity wall, must not be less than 200 mm (8 in) thick. (In Scotland this should be increased to 300 mm (12 in) unless fire-resistant bricks or blocks are used) (Fig. 11.4).

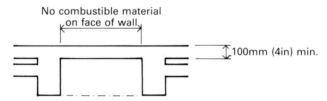

11.4   L3 (2) (c) (i)

L3 (2) (c) (i) If the wall at the back of the fireplace recess is an external wall and there is no external combustible cladding, then the thickness of that wall may be reduced to 100 mm (150 mm in Scotland if fire-resistant bricks or blocks are not used). The back wall of the fireplace must be of solid construction and, in calculating the thickness of the wall, no account may be taken of any of the material such as firebacks or brickettes which may make up the back of an appliance. However, reducing this part of the wall to 100 mm (4 in) is not good practice as it is unlikely to keep out the weather or comply with thermal insulation requirements. In the case of cavity walls, it is always better therefore to maintain the cavity round the back of the fireplace recess (Fig. 11.3).

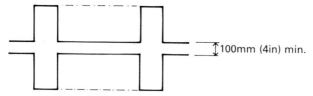

100mm (4in) min.

11.5 L3 (2) (c) (ii)

L3 (2) (c) (ii) Where two fireplaces within the same dwelling are positioned back-to-back, then the dividing wall between the fireplaces should not be less than 100 mm (4 in). (In Scotland this dimension should be 150 mm (6 in) if fire-resistant bricks or blocks are not used) (Fig. 11.5).

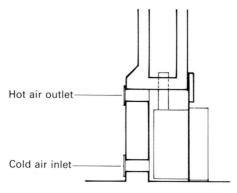

Hot air outlet

Cold air inlet

11.6 L3 (4) (a and b)

L3 (4) (a and b) There should be no openings in the back of a fireplace recess except those which are made to convey convected air through high and low level grilles to a room immediately behind the fireplace. Where such a convector fire is installed then the air ducts must not communicate with the flue (Fig. 11.6).

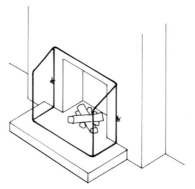

11.7 L2 (5)

L2 (5) When a fire burns directly on a hearth, or an appliance is installed which is an open fire and cannot be used as a closed stove, then provision must be made for securely anchoring a fireguard to the adjoining structure (Fig. 11.7).

Building Regulations for constructional hearths

L2 All fireplaces, roomheaters, closed or open stoves must stand on a constructional hearth. This must be made of solid incombustible material, usually concrete, and should be laid level.

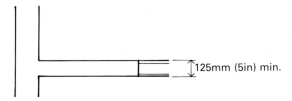

125mm (5in) min.

11.8   L4 (1) (a)

L4 (1) (a) The constructional hearth should be a minimum of 125 mm (5 in) thick. (In Scotland this thickness can include an incombustible finish and if the hearth is laid directly on the ground it can be reduced to 100 mm (4 in) excluding any surface finish (Fig. 11.8).

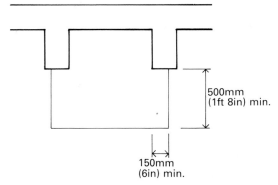

500mm
(1ft 8in) min.

150mm
(6in) min.

11.9   L4 (1) (c)

L4 (1) (c) Where the fireplace is recessed, the constructional hearth must extend to the back of the recess and project not less than 150 mm (6 in) beyond each side of the fireplace opening and extend not less than 500 mm (20 in) from the face of the chimney breast (Fig. 11.9).

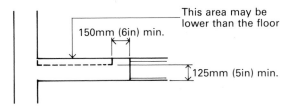

This area may be lower than the floor

150mm (6in) min.

125mm (5in) min.

11.10   L4 (1) (b)

L4 (1) (b and c) Where the constructional hearth adjoins a floor made of combustible material, then a border not less than 150 mm (6 in) must not be lower than the adjoining floor (Fig. 11.10). The area inside this border may be lower than the adjacent floor

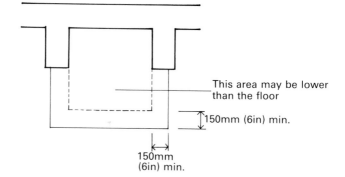

This area may be lower than the floor

150mm (6in) min.

150mm (6in) min.

11.11   L4 (1) (c)

providing the minimum thickness of the hearth, 125 mm (5 in), is maintained (Fig. 11.11).

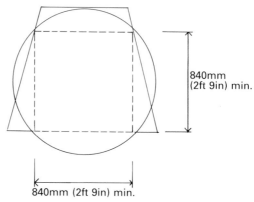

840mm (2ft 9in) min.

11.12   L4 (1) (d)   840mm (2ft 9in) min.

L4 (1) (d) Where a fireplace, stove or boiler is freestanding, the constructional hearth must contain a minimum square of 840 mm (2 ft 9 in) whatever the actual shape of the hearth (Fig. 11.12).

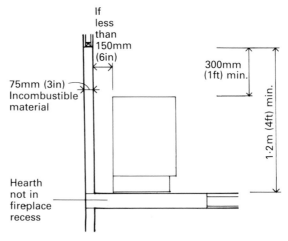

If less than 150mm (6in)

75mm (3in) Incombustible material

300mm (1ft) min.

1·2 m (4ft) min.

Hearth not in fireplace recess

11.13   L5 and M4 (7)

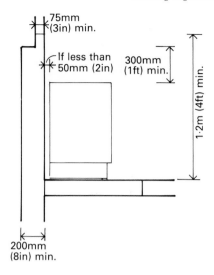

75mm
(3in) min.

If less than
50mm (2in)

300mm
(1ft) min.

1.2m (4ft) min.

200mm
(8in) min.

11.14   M4 (7) (b)

L5 and M4 (7) (b)   If a fireplace, stove or boiler sits on a hearth in front of or beside a wall (as opposed to being in a fireplace recess) the distance between the appliance and any adjacent walls must not be less than 150 mm (6 in) unless the walls are constructed of incombustible material not less than 75 mm (3 in) thick carried up to a height not less than 1.2 m (4 ft 0 in) (Fig. 11.13). The distance from the wall can be reduced, providing the wall is a minimum of 200 mm (8 in) thick of incombustible material. In both cases the walls must be built to the required thickness for at least 300 mm (12 in) above the top of the appliance (Fig. 11.14).

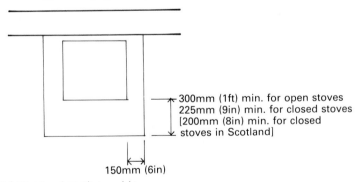

300mm (1ft) min. for open stoves
225mm (9in) min. for closed stoves
[200mm (8in) min. for closed
stoves in Scotland]

150mm (6in)

11.15   L4 (2) (a) and M (4) (a and b)

L4 (2) (a) and M4 (4) (a and b)   No combustible material should be laid on a constructional hearth, such as a continuation of the adjoining floor finish, which would be nearer the base of an appliance than 150 mm (6 in) at the sides and 300 mm (12 in) in front of any appliance which can be operated as an open fire. For closed stoves or boilers the combustible material must not be nearer than 225 mm (9 in). (In Scotland 200 mm (8 in) in front) (Fig. 11.15).

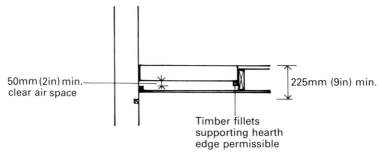

50mm (2in) min. clear air space

225mm (9in) min.

Timber fillets supporting hearth edge permissible

11.16   L4 (3)

L4 (3)   Where a constructional hearth is built into a suspended timber floor, then no combustible material shall be placed under the hearth for a distance of 250 mm (10 in). There are two permitted exceptions to this rule:

Timber fillets supporting the front and side edges of the hearth are allowed and other timbers such as those supporting a ceiling are allowed providing there is a clear air space between them and the underside of the hearth of not less than 50 mm (2 in). (In Scotland, combustible material may be placed under a hearth providing the hearth is a minimum of 250 mm (10 in) thick) (Fig. 11.16).

(In the GLC area, concrete hearths must be cast in-situ in one operation and shall be reinforced to the satisfaction of the District Surveyor. They can be supported if necessary at the outer edges with timber fillets not less than 50 × 38 mm (2 × 1½ in). All shuttering underneath the hearth must be removed).

Also in the GLC area, where a constructional hearth extends less than 400 mm (16 in) from the fire, measured in any direction, then a fixed raised incombustible curb a minimum of 38 mm (1½ in) high should be fixed to overlap the edge of the constructional hearth. The outer edge of this curb should not be less than 300 mm (12 in) from the face of the fire (Fig. 11.17).

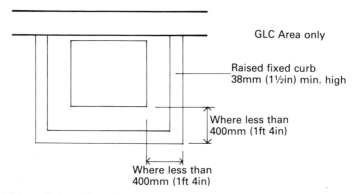

GLC Area only

Raised fixed curb 38mm (1½in) min. high

Where less than 400mm (1ft 4in)

Where less than 400mm (1ft 4in)

11.17   This regulation only applies in the GLC area.

Building Regulations for superimposed hearths

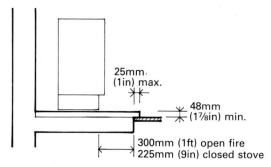

25mm.
(1in) max.

48mm
(1⅞in) min.

300mm (1ft) open fire
225mm (9in) closed stove

11.18   L4 (2) (b) and M4 (3) (c)

L4 (2) (b) and M4 (3) (c) A superimposed hearth is defined by the Building Regulations as 'a hearth not forming part of the structure of a building'. In practice a superimposed hearth is usually installed in order to provide a decorative finish or to raise the level of an existing hearth above the surrounding floor.

A superimposed hearth must be made of incombustible materials, not less than 48 mm (1⅞ in) thick and always be placed wholly or partly upon a constructional hearth.

Any appliance which is placed upon a superimposed hearth must be positioned so that it is wholly over the constructional hearth underneath.

No combustible material should extend under the superimposed hearth more than 25 mm (1 in) or be nearer the base of the appliance than 150 mm (6 in). Nor should the base of an appliance be nearer the edge of a superimposed hearth than the dimensions mentioned in L4 (2) (a) under constructional hearths (Fig. 11.18).

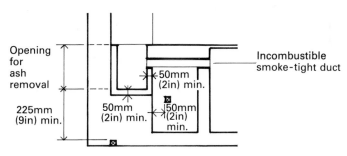

Opening
for
ash
removal

Incombustible
smoke-tight duct

50mm
(2in) min.

225mm
(9in) min.

50mm
(2in) min.

50mm
(2in)
min.

11.19   L4 (4)

L4 (4) Ashpits are permitted within hearths, providing the walls and the bottom of the pit are made of incombustible material not less than 50 mm (2 in) thick. (In Scotland there should be an additional base below this lining of 100 mm (4 in) minimum thickness.) (In the GLC area, the walls and base should be a minimum 125 mm (5 in) thick and, if not on solid ground, should be supported to the satisfaction of the District Surveyor).

No openings are permitted within the pit, except for incombustible smoke-tight airducts and, in external walls only, an opening is permitted in the back wall for ash removal.

No combustible material may be built into the wall less than 225 mm (9 in) below the top of the base of the pit or within 50 mm (2 in) elsewhere beside or below the pit (Fig. 11.19).

Building Regulations for existing hearths

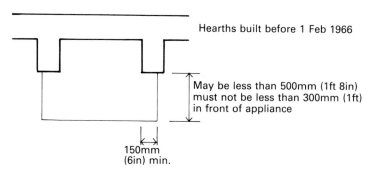

Hearths built before 1 Feb 1966

May be less than 500mm (1ft 8in) must not be less than 300mm (1ft) in front of appliance

150mm (6in) min.

11.20   M4 (3) (b)

M4 (3) (b) Appliances may be installed upon constructional hearths which were built under 'former control' (i.e. constructed before 1 February 1966 before the current Building Regulations were in operation) providing they are a minimum 125 mm (5 in) thick and extend 300 mm (12 in) in front of the appliance and 150 mm (6 in) beyond each side.

In the case of non-recessed fireplaces, the hearth may not be less than 840 mm (2 ft 9 in) square.

In the GLC area, for hearths which are less than 125 mm (5 in) thick, a superimposed hearth, not less than 75 mm (3 in) thick, may be bedded down onto the existing constructional hearth (Fig. 11.20).

Building Regulations for chimneys and flues for Class I appliances

Structural stability

D8 and D15 The structure of a building above the foundations shall be constructed to sustain safely and transmit to the foundations the combined dead load and wind load. The height of chimneys in brick, blocks or concrete which are not otherwise supported by adequate ties should not exceed 4½ times the smallest width dimension of the stack (Fig. 11.21). (This dimension can be six times the smallest width in the GLC area).

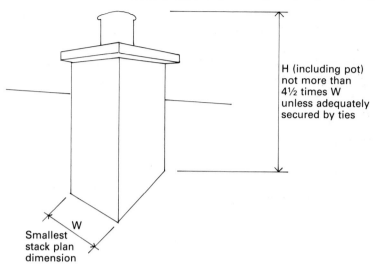

H (including pot)
not more than
4½ times W
unless adequately
secured by ties

W
Smallest
stack plan
dimension

11.21   D8 and D15

Safety in fire

E9 (5)   Chimneys or ducts enclosing flues which pass through or form part of a compartment wall shall be of non-combustible materials, having fire resistance of not less than half the minimum fire resistance required for the wall or floor as laid down in E5 (Fire resistance in elements of structure).

General structural requirements

L2 Flues must be non-combustible, withstand heat, condensation and the products of combustion. They must be positioned to prevent ignition of any part of the building and must prevent products of combustion escaping into the building.

They should be protected from accidental damage and undue danger to persons in or around the building.

They must be accessible for cleaning, either directly from the hearth, through the appliance or with a soot door.

Chimneys

L6 (1) and (2) Flues must be lined with any of the following:

  (a) Clay flue linings to BS 1181:1971;
  (b) rebated and socketed flue linings of kiln-burnt aggregate and high alumina cement;
  (c) clay pipes and fittings to BS 65 and 540 Part 1 1971.

They may also be constructed of concrete flue blocks with inside walls made of kiln-burnt aggregate and high-alumina cement.

All joints between linings and blocks shall be pointed with cement mortar and sockets must point upwards to prevent condensation from the flue leaking into the stack (Fig. 11.22).

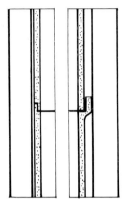

Flue liner sockets uppermost

11.22   L6 (1) and (2)

NB: Flexible metal liners are **not** suitable for solid fuel appliances.

(In Scotland, if the flue is not lined, and the chimneys are less than 200 mm (8 in) thick, then the chimney below the roof must be plastered with a minimum of 7 mm ($\frac{5}{16}$ in) plaster or mortar render).

(In the GLC area, flues should be rendered or plastered inside or lined to the satisfaction of the District Surveyor. Except where a chimney wall is part of the outside of an external wall and the chimney walls are less than 200 mm (8 in) thick they must be rendered up to the height of roof or gutter).

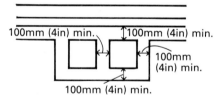

11.23   L6 (3) (a and b)

L6 (3) (a) and (b) The flue shall be surrounded and separated from any other flue by solid material not less than 100 mm (4 in) thick, excluding the thickness of the lining (Fig. 11.23).

(In Scotland, this dimension must be increased to 150 mm (6 in) if fire-resistant bricks or blocks are not used).

(In the GLC area, flues bigger than 0.1 m² (155 in²) must be surrounded by solid walls not less than 200 mm (8 in) thick).

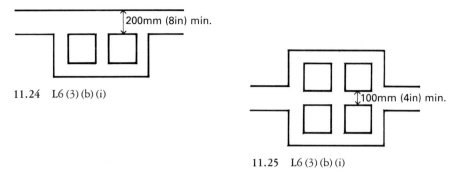

11.24   L6 (3) (b) (i)

11.25   L6 (3) (b) (i)

L6 (3) (b) (i) Where the chimney forms part of wall dividing dwellings then the dividing solid wall must be increased to 200 mm (8 in) below the roof, or in the case of a cavity wall, each leaf shall not be less than 100 mm (4 in) (Fig. 11.24).

(In Scotland these dimensions must be increased to 300 mm (12 in) for solid walls and 150 mm (6 in) for cavity leaves if fire-resistant bricks or blocks are not used).

Where flues are back-to-back on a wall separating buildings, the wall between the flues must not be less than 100 mm (4 in) thick (Fig. 11.25).

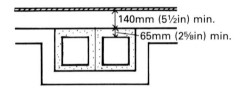

11.26   L6 (3) (b) (ii)

L6 (3) (b) (ii) In chimneys constructed of concrete flue blocks, no vertical joints are permitted to adjoin the flues.

When a concrete block flue is in an external wall and there is a distance of not less than 140 mm (5½ in) between the inside of the flue blocks and any combustible cladding, the walls of the flue blocks may be reduced to a minimum of 65 mm (2⅝ in) (Fig. 11.26).

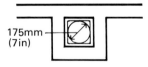

11.27   L6 (4)

L6 (4) Flues connecting to a fireplace recess must maintain a minimum diameter of 175 mm (7 in) except for a restriction to form a throat (Fig. 11.27).

(This dimension is a minimum of 150 mm (6 in) in the GLC area)

Note however CP 131 recommends that a flue for an open fire should not be less than 185 mm (7⅜ in) square or 200 mm (8 in) circular diameter.

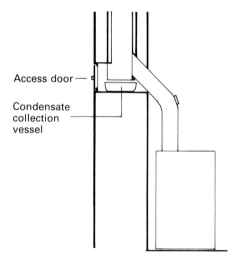

Access door

Condensate
collection
vessel

11.28   L6 (5) (a)

L6 (5) (a) Flues which do not connect to a fireplace recess (but instead to an appliance by means of a flue pipe) must terminate at the bottom with an access door for inspection and cleaning and be capable of holding a vessel to collect condensation (Fig. 11.28).

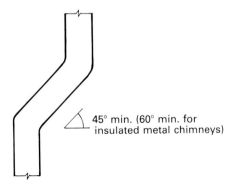

45° min. (60° min. for
insulated metal chimneys)

11.29   L6 (6) and L22 (2) (c)

L6 (6) and L22 (2) (c)   Offsets in flues should not be less than 45° to the horizontal and 60° for insulated metal chimneys except where necessary to connect the flue to the appliance (Fig. 11.29).

(In GLC area flues at less than 45° must be fitted with a soot door in an iron frame).

Flue pipes for Class I appliances

L7 (1) and (3) No flue pipe may pass through any floor, internal wall, partition or roof space other than the space between the roof covering and the ceiling – i.e. rafters or roof joists.

144

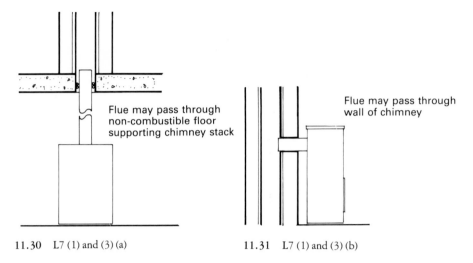

11.30   L7 (1) and (3) (a)   11.31   L7 (1) and (3) (b)

Exceptions are:
(a) a flue pipe may pass through a non-combustible floor supporting a chimney stack,
    to discharge vertically into the bottom of a flue (Fig. 11.30);
(b) a flue pipe may pass through a wall which is the wall of a chimney (Fig. 11.31).

L7 (2) The cross-sectional area of a flue pipe shall not be less than the cross-sectional
area of the outlet of the appliance.

Flue pipe materials for Class I appliances

L8 (a) and (c)   Flue pipes may be made of cast iron to BS 41:1973 or mild steel not less
than 4.75 mm (³⁄₁₆ in) thick, or any other material deemed to satisfy Regulation L2 (1)
(a) (i).
   (In the GLC area, flue pipes can be of mild steel a minimum of 3 mm (⅛ in) thick or of
precast concrete units with refractory linings not less than 64 mm (2½ in) thick. They
can also be of heavy duty asbestos cement providing they are not nearer than 1.8 m (5 ft
11 in) from the appliance.)
   A flue pipe serving a freestanding open fire, which cannot be used as a closed stove,

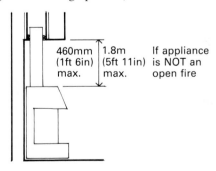

460mm 1.8m   If appliance
(1ft 6in) (5ft 11in) is NOT an
max.   max.   open fire

11.32   L8 (c)

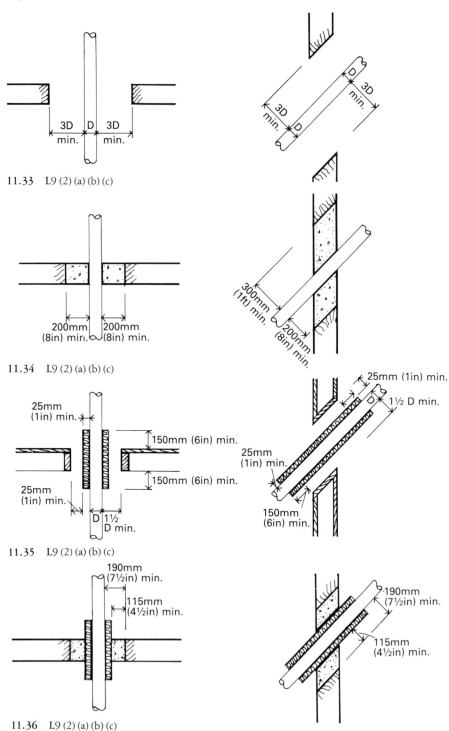

11.33   L9 (2) (a) (b) (c)

11.34   L9 (2) (a) (b) (c)

11.35   L9 (2) (a) (b) (c)

11.36   L9 (2) (a) (b) (c)

may be made of sheet steel not less than 1.2 mm thick providing the distance between the appliance and the chimney is not more than 460 mm (18 in) (Fig. 11.32).

None of the conditions applying to chimneys apply to the chimney pot or terminal.

Placing and shielding of flue pipes for Class I appliances

L9 (1) A flue pipe must be so placed and shielded as to prevent ignition of any part of any building.

L9 (2) (a) (b) (c) No combustible materials are permitted nearer than three times the outside diameter of the flue pipe, when it passes through an external wall or roof (Fig. 11.33), unless separated by non-combustible material not less than 200 mm (8 in) thick and 300 mm (12 in) thick above the pipe in a wall (Fig. 11.34), or enclosed in a sleeve of metal or asbestos cement which projects not less than 150 mm (6 in) above and below the roof or wall and has not less than 25 mm (1 in) non-combustible insulation packed between the pipe and the sleeve. Where the flue pipe passes through a hollow combustible roof or wall, there must be a space not less than 25 mm (1 in) between the outer face of the sleeve, and it must not be less than one-and-a-half times the external diameter of the pipe from the combustible roof or wall (Fig. 11.35).

However, where a flue pipe passes through a solid roof or floor, the distance between the outside of the pipe and any combustible material forming part of the roof or wall must be not less than 190 mm (7½ in) and the space between the sleeve must be filled with solid non-combustible not less than 115 mm (4½ in) thick (Fig. 11.36).

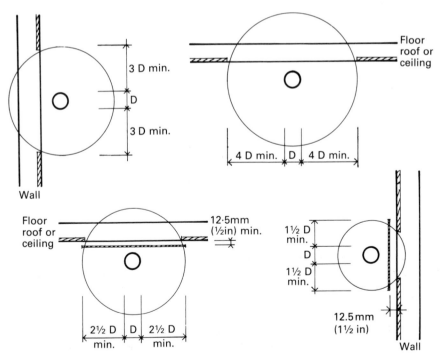

11.37   L9 (3) (a) and (4) (a)

L9 (3) (a) and (4) (a) A flue pipe shall not be nearer to any combustible material in a wall than three times its external diameter, or four times its external diameter in a floor, roof or ceiling (Fig. 11.37). This dimension can be reduced to one and a half times its external diameter in a wall and two and a half times the external diameter in a floor, roof or ceiling if the combustible material is protected by a non-combustible shield placed with an air space between the shield and the face of the wall or roof of not less than 12.5 mm (½ in).

Proximity of combustible materials for Class I appliances

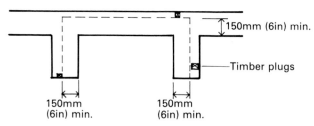

11.38   L10 (1)

L10 (1) No combustible material shall be placed in any chimney or the inside face of a fireplace recess nearer than 150 mm (6 in) for timber plugs or 200 mm (8 in) for any other material (Fig. 11.38).

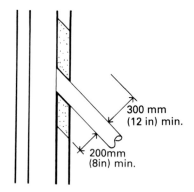

11.39   L10 (2)

L10 (2) A flue pipe passing through a chimney wall shall be separated from any combustible material placed in that wall by solid non-combustible material for a distance of not less than 300 mm (12 in) above the flue and 200 mm (8 in) beside or below the flue (Fig. 11.39).

L10 (3) Where a flue pipe discharges into the bottom of a flue in a chimney supported by a floor or roof, it shall be separated from any combustible material by solid non-combustible material not less than 200 mm (8 in) all round (Fig. 11.40).

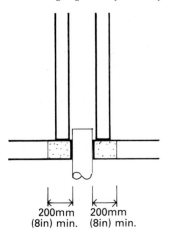

200mm   200mm
(8in) min.   (8in) min.

11.40   L10 (3)

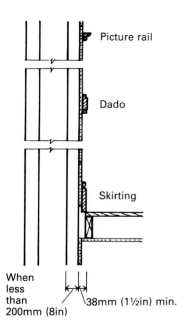

Picture rail

Dado

Skirting

When
less
than
200mm (8in)

38mm (1½in) min.

11.41   L10 (4)

L10 (4) Where the walls of a chimney are less than 200 mm (8 in) thick, no combustible material, other than a floorboard, skirting board, dado rail, picture rail, mantelshelf or architrave shall be placed nearer than 38 mm (1½ in) to the outer surface of the chimney (Fig. 11.41).

L11 No openings are permitted in flues or flue pipes except for a soot door for cleaning and inspection, an air inlet capable of being closed, a draught stabiliser or explosion door, all to be positioned in the same room as the appliance.

L12 No flue or flue pipe shall communicate with more than one room or internal space in a building except for a soot door.

Outlets of flues for Class 1 appliances

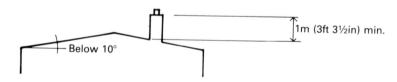

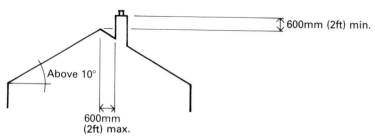

11.42   L13 (a)

L13 (a) The top of a chimney or flue pipe, excluding any pot or terminal, shall project not less than 1 m (3 ft 3½ in) above the highest point of contact between the chimney and the roof. Where the pitch on both sides of the roof is not less than 10° to the horizontal and the chimney is within 600 mm (2 ft) of the ridge, the top of the stack shall not be less than 600 mm (2 ft) above the ridge (Fig. 11.42).

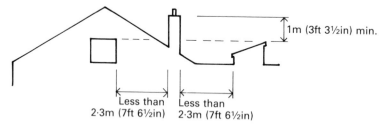

11.43   L13 (b) and (c)

L13 (b) and (c)   The top of a chimney must not be less than 1 m (3 ft 3½ in) above the top of any opening light, ventilator, or part of a building (other than a roof, parapet wall or other chimney) which is less than 2.3 m (7 ft 6½ in) on plan, away from the top of the chimney (Fig. 11.43).

L22 (1)(2)(a) and (b)   Insulated metal chimneys must comply with L2 (4) and (6), L6 (4) and (7), L11, L12, L13 and must be constructed of components complying with

150

BS 4543:1976. No joints are allowed between components within the thickness of any wall, floor, ceiling or roof.

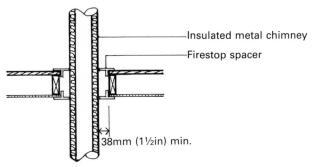

—Insulated metal chimney

—Firestop spacer

38mm (1½in) min.

11.44   L22 (2) (d) and (e)

L22 (2) (d) and (e)   No combustible material shall be placed nearer to the outer surface of the chimney than 38 mm (1½ in) as BS 4543:1976 or the manufacturer's specified clearance (Fig. 11.44). The chimney shall be readily accessible for inspection and replacement throughout its length.

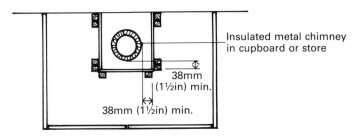

Insulated metal chimney in cupboard or store

38mm (1½in) min.

38mm (1½in) min.

11.45   L22 (2) (f)

L22 (2) (f) If any part of an insulated metal chimney is situated within a cupboard or storage space, it shall be enclosed by a removable, imperforate casing, with a clear space between the outside of the flue and the casing of not less than 38 mm (1½ in) or the manufacturer's specified clearance, with no combustible material inside the casing (Fig. 11.45).

L22 (2) (g) No part of the chimney shall pass through or be attached to any building other than the building in which the appliance served by the chimney is situated.

(In Scotland, where an insulated metal chimney is more than 1.8 m (5 ft 11 in) above the roof, the chimney shall be braced to the roof).

Class I appliances

M4 (9) Class I appliances shall discharge into a flue in a chimney or a flue pipe which complies with part L (excluding Regulation L6 for chimneys built before 1976).

M4 (10)   The flue into which the appliance discharges shall serve no other appliance, except for the installation of two solid-fuel or oil-burning appliances (i.e. a cooker and an independent boiler) where both appliances are in the same room, are closed slow-burning appliances and their combined rating does not exceed 45 kW (154 000 Btu/h) and the cross-sectional area of the flue is not less than the area of the larger of the two flue connections.

M4 (2) and M7 Provision must be made for adequate supply of combustion air to ensure efficient operation and proper discharge from the appliance into the flue. In practice, opening window and natural draughts are generally sufficient for appliances up to 12 kW (41 000 Btu/hs).

British Standards

The British Standards Institution (BSI) aims to set down minimum standards of quality and performance for a multiplicity of material and products – and to set down guidelines indicating desired levels of performance for components and assemblies.

It does this by producing *British Standards* which describe the dimensions, properties and performance of a material or product and *Codes of Practice* which describe the methods which should be used to install or assemble such products.

Where British Standards or Codes of Practice are referred to in the Building Regulations, then they become mandatory – otherwise they are merely advisory.

A list of British Standards and Codes of Practice which refer to fireplaces, chimneys and their components follows. Those marked with an asterisk are specifically mentioned in the Building Regulations.

   11.46   British Standards Institution Kitemark

The British Standards Institution is owner of the *Kitemark*, a registered trade mark showing a kite with the number of the relevant standard. This mark on an appliance, fireback, fireguard or similar product will assure the consumer that the goods have been produced to a standard (Fig. 11.46).

Appliances

BS 3376:1961   Open fires with convection with or without boiler.
BS 3377:1969   Back boilers for use with domestic solid-fuel appliances.
BS 3378:1972   Roomheaters burning solid fuel.
BS 4834:1972   Inset open fires without convection.
BS 5258:1980   Decorative gas log and other fuel-effect appliances.
(Part 12)

Appliance accessories

BS 1251:1970	Open fireplace components (firebacks, surrounds, hearths, throat restrictors and lintels).
BS 2788:1956	Fireguards for solid-fuel fires.
BS 3140:1967	Nursery type fireguards.
BS 3248:1960	Sparkguards for solid-fuel fires.
BS 3328:1961	Domestic gas pokers and portable underbar ignition burners.

Chimneys

*BS 4543:1976	Factory-made insulated chimneys.
BS 1294:1946	Soot doors for domestic buildings.

Flue linings

*BS 65 and 540:1971	Clay drain and sewer pipes including surface water pipes and fittings.
*BS 1181:1971	Clay flue linings and flue terminals.

Flue pipes

*BS 41:1973	Cast iron spigot and socket flue or smoke pipes and fittings.
*BS 835:1973	Asbestos cement flue pipes and fittings – heavy quality.

*denotes Standards specifically mentioned in the Building Regulations.

Codes of Practice

These are available from the British Standards Institution.

CP 403: 1974	Installation of domestic heating and cooking appliances burning solid fuel.
CP 121:1973	Walling (includes recommendations for damp-proof courses and flashings for chimneys).
CP 131:1974	Chimneys and flues for domestic appliances burning solid fuel.
BS 5854:1980	Code of Practice for flues and flue structures in buildings.

British Standards and Codes of Practice are published by and can be bought from:

British Standards Institution
2 Park Street
London W1A 2BS
Telephone: 01–629 9000

They can also be bought from HMSO Bookshops.

Chapter 12

ADVICE

Solid Fuel Advisory Service

The Solid Fuel Advisory Service (SFAS) is a nationwide organisation set up in 1973 and financed jointly by the National Coal Board, the independent producers of solid smokeless fuels and coal traders.

Its purpose is to promote the sale of solid fuels and appliances to the domestic market, and to offer expert advice to architects and builders.

Every year SFAS publishes a paper called *Approved Domestic Solid Fuel Appliances*. This is a list of appliances currently in production which have been approved under the Domestic Solid Fuel Appliances Approval Scheme for the National Coal Board. For purposes of approval, appropriate British Standards Specifications are used. To qualify for a grant in a Smoke Control Area, an 'approved' appliance must normally be selected.

The SFAS headquarters is in the National Coal Board Building, Hobart Place, London SW1. There are seven regions which have some 51 offices. In Northern Ireland there is an equivalent organisation, the *Coal Advisory Service* which has four offices. (See page 162 for addresses).

In addition to the regional offices, there is a network of *Living Fire Centres*. Unlike the Gas and Electricity Boards, the National Coal Board does not have High Street showrooms, mainly because consumers do not pay their solid fuel bills directly to the Board, but to coal merchants. The gas and electricity showrooms provide a place where people can pay bills and at the same time view and buy new appliances. Living Fire Centres therefore provide a similar service but are generally housed within existing Builders Merchants' or Coal Merchants' premises. In 1980 there were some 138 such centres and their addresses can be obtained from the SFAS, Hobart Place, London SW1.

Householders can obtain free technical advice from the regional SFAS offices, including technical publications about the various fuels available, and the design and installation of chimneys and appliances.

National Fireplace Council

This council was set up in 1970 by the Fireplace Manufacturers' Association, the Ceramic Fireplace Tile Council, The National Federation of Builders and Plumbers' Merchants and the National Coal Board.

One of the aims was to provide fireplace centres and showrooms in cities and towns throughout the United Kingdom. These are generally housed in Builders' Merchants, Manufacturers' showrooms and Home Improvement Centres. In 1980 there were 146 *National Fireplace Centres* and 52 *National Fireplace Showrooms*, which are smaller establishments. The centres should have a large number of fireplaces on display and staff who can give advice on fireplace design and installation. For addresses consult the National Fireplace Council, PO Box 35, Stoke-on-Trent, Tel: 0782 44311.

Manufacturers, importers and suppliers

Listed below, in alphabetical order, are some of the principal British manufacturers and importers of appliances.

For local showrooms and suppliers, consult the Solid Fuel Advisory Service for the addresses of their regional offices and Living Fire Centres. Consult also the yellow pages of telephone directories for centres which specialise in supplying fireplace appliances. Consult local builders' merchants for the supply of items connected with building fireplace recesses and chimneys.

Appliance chests
Park Sectional
Rite-Vent
Selkirk Metalbestos
Ash carriers
Nymak 'Trapa'
Winchwing 'Tippy'

Barbecues
Odell
Bellows
Kingsworthy
La Belle Cheminée

Canopies – hoods
Kingsley
Mansfield Engineering
Pearson
Smellie
Valmar

Chestnut roasters
Beardmore
Hyders
Chimney cowls and terminals
Colt
Ensor
Kraemer
OH Ltd
Red Bank   'Marcone',
                          'Popular'
Chimney fans
Aidelle Products
Strax   'Exhausto'
Chimney pots
Ensor
Marley (True Flue)
Red Bank
Chimneys — precast block
Keddy
Kolind
Park Sectional
Taylor and Portway
Thermoflue

Chimneys — prefabricated insulated
Insulated Chimneys
ITT Reznor
Park Sectional
Rega Metal
Rite-Vent
Selkirk Metalbestos
System Chimneys
Williams

Coal bunkers
Banbury Homes and Gardens
Compton Buildings
Johnson
Marley
Reinforced Concrete Construction

Electric firelighters
Pifco

Fenders
Acquisitions
Beardmore
Country Style
Valmar

Firebacks – cast iron
Beardmore
Interoven
Kingsworthy
La Belle Cheminée
Smellie

Firebacks – clay
Hewitt

Firebaskets
Beardmore
Bell
Classic Garden
Hyders
Interoven
Kingsworthy
Ouzledale
Petit Roque
Renzland
Rotheriron
Smellie
T. I. Parkray

Fire curtains
Galleon
Puritan Forge

Fire dogs
Beardmore
Classic Garden

Interoven
La Belle Cheminée
Kingsworthy
Rotheriron

Fireguards and sparkguards
Baker

Fire irons
Beardmore
Bell
Classic Garden
Hyders
Kingsworthy
Odell
Ouzledale
Rotheriron

Fireplace surrounds
(further names are available from the National
Fireplace Council — address on page 162)
Acquisitions
Bell
Carved Pine Mantelpieces
Galleon
La Belle Cheminée
Marble Hill
Minsterstone
Patrick
Pearson
Petit Roque
Quiligotti
Verine
Victoria Stone

Fires – ducted warm-air inset open fires

Fosse Warmair	'Deville'
Keddy	'Impuls air'
Strax	'Dovre'

Fires – fan-assisted inset open

Grahamston	'Queen Fan-Fire'
Redcar	'Atlas Kwikglo'
T.I. Parkray	'Parkray Fan Fire'

Fires — freestanding open

Bell	'Canopy', 'Central Canopy', 'Pico-Bell'
Dunsley	'Condor'
Glynwed Appliances	'Rayburn Open Fire'
Keddy	'Windfire'
Kingsley	'Granada', 'Monaco', 'San Remo', 'Toledo'
Ocees	'Acorn'
Ouzledale	'Firemaster 78'
T.I. Parkray	'Parkray No 2a'
Wonderfire	'Jalco'

Fires — inset convectors

Glynwed Foundries	'Convectaflow'
Jetmaster	'Universal', 'Extra'

Keddy	'Superfire'
Logfires	'Heatstream'
Modern Fires	'Scan Unit'
Norcem	'Jøtul insert stove'
Tortoise	'Firebox'

Fires — inset open (many can be supplied with back boilers)

Bell	'Bell'
Dunsley	'Enterprise', 'Firefly', 'Lofire'
Glynwed Appliances	'Lexham', 'Lowburn', 'Rayburn', 'Sofono'
Grahamston	'Queen', 'Queenette'
Interoven	'Cokeglo', 'Virgil'
Jones and Campbell	'Tor'
Ouzledale	'Firemaster'
Redcar	'Atlas', 'Valiant'
Smellie	'Firex'
Smith and Wellstood	'Esse Bramble', 'Esse Fleur
T.I. Parkray	'Parkray Paragon', 'Parkray Paramount'
Trianco Redfyre	'Trianco Redfyre 4a, 55, Hybac'

Fires — inset open with underfloor duct and deep ashpit (Hole-in-the-wall fires)

Baxi	'Burnall'
Bell	'Bell Supaheat'
Dunsley	'Dunsley Underfloor'
Grahamston	'Queen Sunk Fire'
Kingsley	'Hole-in-the-Wall'
Ouzledale	'Firemaster Superdraught'
Smellie	'Firex'

Firescreens
Beardmore
Galleon
Hyders
Kingsworthy
Renzland
Rotheriron

Firestools and frets
Dudley

Flue liners
Keddy
Kolind
Marley (True Flue)
Park Sectional
Red Bank
Rite-Vent
Williams

Flue lining systems for existing flues
Nu-Flu
Supaflu

Flue pipes
Kraemer
Marley (True Flue)
Park Sectional
Rega Metal
Rite-Vent
System Chimneys
Williams

Fuel buckets, hods and cradles
Baker
Beardmore
Bell
Classic Garden
Hyders
Renzland

Gas fuel effect fires
Kohlangaz
La Belle Cheminée
Real Flame
Therm-o-Flame
Wonderfire

Gas pokers
Baxi

Newspaper brick presses
Watts

Raft lintels
Park Sectional
Red Bank

Roomheaters – see Stoves

Soot doors
Dudley
Marley (True Flue)

Stoves — box (Closed box-shaped stoves generally for woodburning, some are multi-fuel)

Broomside	'Cherry'
Jetmaster	'Coal Burner'
Modern Fires	'Bekka' 'Lange'
Norcem	'Jøtul 201 Turbo'
Quebb	'Quebb'
Strax	'Ulefos'
Sykes	'Leda'

Stoves — open (Woodburning and multi-fuel)

Bell	'Franklin'
Broomside	'Franklin'
Franco Belge	'Brule Bois'
Fosse Warmair	'Deville'
Glynwed Foundries	'Darby', 'Wenlock'
Hunter	'Midi', 'Traditional', 'Select'
Interoven	'Goodwood', 'Grenadier', 'Rais', 'Rondo', 'Sovereign'
Jetmaster	'Convector Stove'
Keeping	'Woodwarm'
Logfires	'Logfires'
Modern Fires	'Caldo', 'Halken', 'Lange'
Marley Marketing	'Vermont'
Norcem	'Jøtul'
Odell	'Federal'
Petal Agencies	'Scan'
Smith and Wellstood	Esse– 'Courtier', 'Dolphin', 'Dragon', 'Flame', 'Queen',
Spencer	'Grand Select', 'President', 'Princess', 'Senator', 'Sherwood', 'Sterling' 'Surdiac'
Strax	'Ulefos'
Sykes	'Astoria Rondo', 'Godin Colonial'
Thorpe	'Thorpeman Villager'
Tortoise	'Grand Select'
Trianco Redfyre	'International', 'Forester'
Waterford	'Waterford'
Wells, A J	'Beacon', 'Charnwood'
Wells, J and J L	'Countryman'
Woodman	'Woodman'
Yeoman	'Yeoman'

Stoves — roomheaters (Closed stoves for solid fuel)

Broomside	'Bermuda'
Brownlow	'Chappee'
Crown	'Montrose'
Davies	'Davey Sapphire'
Franco Belge	'Franco Belge'
Glynwed Appliances	'Rayburn'
Grahamston	'Queen Heater'
Hunter	'Reliant'
Smith and Wellstood	'Esse Elite', 'Esse Bontesse'
Sykes	'Godin'

Taylor and Portway	'Portway Brick Central Unit'
T.I. Parkray	'Parkray Coalmaster', 'Everglow', 'G, GL and GF'
Trianco Redfyre	'Trianco Redfyre TRH', 'Housemaster', 'Tallboy'

Stoves — studio or workshop (Tall closed stoves generally for solid fuel)

Broomside	'Arctic', 'Epping', 'Nevada'
Hunter	'Poppy'
Interoven	'Cosi Comfort'
Modern Fires	'Lange'
Norcem	'Jøtul 507'
Smith and Wellstood	'Romesse'
Strax	'Ulefos'
Sykes	'Godin', 'Canon'
Tortoise	'Tortoise'
Trianco Redfyre	'Studio' (Pither), 'Warm Morning'

Throat restrictors and dampers
Baxi
Dudley
Glynwed Appliances
Magni Reflector

Throat units and lintels
Hewitt
Marley (True Flue)
Park Sectional
Red Bank

Woodburning stoves — see Stoves

Addresses – Manufacturers, importers and suppliers

Acquisitions Fireplaces Ltd, 269 Camden High Street, London
NW1   01 485 4955
Agaheat Appliances, (see Glynwed Appliances Ltd)
Aidelle Products, Lancaster Road, High Wycombe, Bucks   0494 25252

Baker, George Ltd, 68 Cecil Street, Birmingham   021 359 3552
Banbury Homes and Gardens, PO Box 11, Banbury, Oxon   0295 52500
Baxi Heating, PO Box 52, Bamber Bridge, Preston, Lancs   0772 36201
Beardmore, J. D. and Co. Ltd, 3 Percy Street, London W1   01 637 7041
Bell, A. and Co. Ltd, Kingsthorpe, Northampton   0604 712505
Broomside Foundry Co. Ltd, Bonnybridge, Stirlingshire   032481 4122
Brownlow, Colin and Co., 13 Station Road, Egham, Surrey   0784 33595

Carved Pine Mantelpieces Ltd, High Street,
Dorchester-on-Thames, Oxon   0865 340028
Classic Garden Furniture, Audley Avenue, Newport, Salop   0952 813311
Coalbrookdale Co., Coalbrook, Telford, Salop   0952 453395
Colt W H (London) Ltd, New Lane, Havant, Hants   0705 451111
Compton Buildings Ltd, Fenny Compton, Nr Leamington Spa,
Warwicks.   029577 291
Country Style Ltd, 36 Normandy Way, Bodmin, Cornwall   0208 3639
Crown Foundry Co. Ltd, Liliput Road, Brackmills, Northampton   0604 62215

Davies and Pritchard Ltd, New Road, New Inn, Pontypool, Gwent   04955 4336
Dudley, Thomas Ltd, PO Box 28, Dudley, West Midlands   021 557 5411
Dunsley Heating Appliances Co. Ltd, Fearnought, Holmfirth,
Huddersfield, Yorks   048489 2635

Ensor Sales Ltd, Pool Works, Woodville, Burton-upon-Trent,
Staffs   0283 217921
Esse (see Smith and Wellstood Ltd)

Franco Belge Heating Ltd, Oyster Lane, Byfleet, Weybridge,
Surrey   0932 55837
Fosse Warmair Ltd, 17 Lisle Avenue, Kidderminster, Worcs   0562 743634

Galleon-Claygate Ltd, 216 Red Lion Road, Tolworth, Surbiton,
Surrey   01 397 3456
Glynwed Appliances Ltd, PO Box 30, Ketley, Telford, Salop   0952 51177
Glynwed Foundries Ltd, Coalbrookdale, Telford, Salop   0952 453395
Grahamston Iron Co., PO Box 5, Gowan Avenue, Falkirk,
Stirlingshire   0324 22661

Hewitt, J. and Son Ltd, Fenton, Stoke-on-Trent, Staffs   0782 47151
Hunter and Son (Mells) Ltd, Frome, Somerset   0373 812545
Hyders Ltd, Plaxtol, Sevenoaks, Kent   0732 810215

Insulated Chimneys Ltd, Station Road, Donnington, Telford,
Salop   0952 606421
Interoven Ltd, 70–72 Fearnley Street, Watford, Herts   0923 46761
ITT Reznor, Park Farm Road, Folkestone, Kent   0303 59141

Jetmaster Fires Ltd, Winnall Manor Road, Winnall, Winchester,
Hants   0962 51641
Johnson, G. Bros Ltd, Station Road, Donnington, Telford, Salop   0952 606421

Jones and Campbell Ltd, Torwood Factory, Larbert, Stirlingshire,
Scotland   0324 562114

Keeping, S. Ltd, Bridge Street, Uffculme, Cullompton, Devon   0884 40847
Keddy Home Improvements Ltd, 198 High Street, Egham, Surrey   0784 37357
Kingsley Patent Fire Company Ltd, Century Street, Hanley,
Stoke-on-Trent, Staffs.   0782 22242
Kingsworthy Foundry Co. Ltd, Kingsworthy, Winchester, Hants   0962 883776
Kohlangaz Fire Co. Ltd. Whessoe Road, Darlington, Co Durham   0325 55438
Kolind, K E and Co., Burt Axon, Castle Hill Lane, Burley, Hants   04253 3309
Kraemer, George and Co. Ltd. Upper Evingar Road, Whitchurch,
Hants   025682 2162

La Belle Cheminée Ltd, 85 Wigmore Street, London W1   01 486 7486
Logfires, 4 Brighton Road, Horsham, West Sussex   0403 56227

Magni Reflector Co. Ltd, 10 Market Road, Chichester, Sussex   0243 83279
Mansfield Engineering Co. Ltd, The Forge, Bath Road,
Kiln Green, Reading, Berks   073522 3866
Marble Hill Gallery, 72 Richmond Road, Twickenham, Middx   01 892 1488
Marley Buildings Ltd (True Flue Division), Shurdington, Nr
Cheltenham, Glos.   0242 862551
Minsterstone Fireplaces, Station Road, Ilminster, Somerset   04605 2277
Modern Fires (Mitcham), 50 Brighton Road, Salfords, Redhill,
Surrey   02934 3924
Morley Marketing, Victoria Maltings, Broadmeads, Ware, Herts   0920 67554

Norcem (UK) Ltd, Old Bath Road, Charvil, Reading, Berks   0734 340223
Nu-Flu Ltd, Freeholdland, Pontypool, Gwent   04955 57246
Nymak Ltd, 178a London Road, Guildford, Surrey   0483 32826

Ocees Components and Structures Ltd, 49 Knightsbridge Court,
Sloane Street, London SW1   01 235 1453
Odell, Frank Ltd, 43 Broad Street, Teddington, Middx   01 977 8158
OH Ltd, Avon Centre, Wallingford Road, Kingsbridge, Devon   0548 2053
Ouzledale Foundry Co. Ltd, PO Box 4, Barnoldswick, Colne, Lancs   0282 813235

Parkray (see T. I. Parkray Ltd)
Park Sectional Insulating Co. Ltd, 244 Romford Road,
Forest Gate, London E7   01 534 7695
Patrick Fireplaces, Guildford Road, Farnham, Surrey   0252 722345
Pearson, Roger, Wentworth Street, Birdwell, Barnsley S. Yorks   0226 745129
Petal Agencies Ltd, Broad Chalke, Nr Salisbury, Wilts   072278 338
Petit Roque Ltd, 5a New Road, Croxley Green, Rickmansworth,
Herts   0923 720968
Pifco Ltd, Millett House, The Hyde, London NW9   01 205 1164
Pither (see Trianco Redfyre Ltd)
Puritan Forge, The, 135 Notting Hill Gate, London W11   01 221 1067

Quebb Stoves, Alton Road, Ross-on-Wye, Herefordshire   0989 63656
Quillingotti, A. and Co. Ltd, Newby Road, Hazel Grove,
Stockport, Cheshire   061 483 1451

Rayburn (see Glynwed Appliances Ltd)
Real Flame, 80 New Kings Road, London SW6   01 731 2704
Red Bank Manufacturing Co. Ltd, Measham, Burton-upon-Trent,
Staffs   0530 70333

Redcar Boilers and Tanks, Redcar Road, Marske, Redcar, Cleveland	0642 470231
Rega Metal Products Ltd, 6 Eldon Way, Biggleswade, Beds	0767 312996
Renzland, H. and Co. Ltd, London Road, Copford, Colchester, Essex	0206 210212
Reinforced Concrete Construction Co. Ltd, Delph Road, Brierley Hill, W. Midlands	0384 78611
Rite-Vent Ltd, Armstrong Industrial Estate, Washington, Tyne and Wear	0632 461150
Rotheriron, Mount Pleasant, Jarvis Brook, Crowborough, E. Sussex	08926 61677
Selkirk Metalbestos, 10 Lower Grosvenor Place, London SW1	01 828 7226
Smellie, James Ltd, Stafford Street, Dudley, W Midlands	0384 52320
Smith and Wellstood Ltd, Bonnybridge, Stirlingshire	032 481 2171
Spencer, Philip, Stoves Ltd, Cherrycourt Way, Leighton Buzzard, Beds	0525 375048
Strax Distribution Ltd, 41b Brecknock Road, London N7	01 485 7056
Supaflu, 175 Kings Road, Kingston upon Thames, Surrey	01 549 0801
Sykes, Ellis and Son Ltd, Victoria Works, Howard Street, Stockport, Cheshire	061477 5626
System Chimneys Ltd, 3a Waterloo Place, High Street, Crowthorne, Berks	03446 2889
Taylor and Portway Ltd, Rosemary Lane, Halstead, Essex	07874 2551
Therm-O-Flame Ltd, Boston Road, Holbeach, Lincs	0406 22309
Thermoflue Ltd, 33 High Street, Cowbridge, South Glamorgan	04463 4639
Thorpe, Simon Ltd, New Road, Newcastle Emlyn, Dyfed	0239 710100
T. I. Parkray Ltd, Park Foundry, Belper, Derby	077382 3741
Tortoise Stoves, Vale Rise, Tonbridge, Kent	0732 362233
Trianco Redfyre Ltd, Thorncliffe, Chapeltown, Sheffield, S. Yorks	07415 61221
True Flue Ltd (see Marley Buildings Ltd)	
Valmar Engineering, 30 North Street, Carshalton, Surrey	01 669 7744
Verine Products and Co., Goldhanger, Maldon, Essex	0621 88611
Victoria Stone, W. B. Ltd, 79 Saint Johns Road, Tunbridge Wells, Kent	0892 41337
Waterford Stoves Ltd, New Cut Lane, Industrial Estate, Woolston, Warrington, Cheshire	0925 815717
Watts of Calcot, Environment House, Bath Road, Calcot, Berks	0734 411646
Wells A. J. and Sons, Westminster Lane, Newport, Isle of Wight	0983 527552
Wells J. and J. L. Ltd, Wellington Street, Syston, Leics	0533 607050
Williams J. Ltd, Berry Hill Industrial Estate, Droitwich, Worcs	0905 779222
Winchwing Ltd, Chase Side, Ross-on-Wye, Herefordshire	0989 2036
Wonderfire Ltd, 99 Queen's Road, Clifton, Bristol, Avon	0272 311172
Woodman Stoves Ltd, Unit 6, Cibyn Industrial Estate, Caernarfon	0286 3772
Yeoman Stoves, Longdown, Exeter, Devon	039281 259

Organisations

Approved Coal Merchants Scheme, 2 Turpin Lane London SE 10	01 853 0787
Association of British Solid Fuel Appliance Manufacturers,	
Fleming House, Renfrew Street, Glasgow	041 332 0826
British Flue and Chimney Manufacturers Association,	
Unit 3, Phoenix House, Phoenix Way, Heston, Middx	01 629 9000
British Standards Institution, 2 Park Street, London W 1	01 629 9000
Building Centre, The, 26 Store Street, London WC 1	01 637 1022
Design Centre, The, 28 Haymarket, London SW 1	01 839 8000
National Coal Board, Hobart House, Grosvenor Place, London SW 1	01 235 2020
National Fireplace Council, PO Box 35, Stoke-on-Trent, Staffs	0782 44311
Royal Institute of British Architects, 66 Portland Place, London W 1	01 590 5533
Solid Fuel Advisory Service, Hobart House, Grosvenor Place,	
London SW 1	01 235 2020
Regional Offices:	
Scotland: Green Park, Green End, Edinburgh	031 6641461
North: Coal House, Team Valley Trading Estate, Gateshead, Tyne and Wear	0632 878822
Yorkshire: Consort House, Waterdale, Doncaster, S. Yorks	0302 66611
North West: Anderton House, Newton Road, Lowton, Warrington, Cheshire	094 67312
Midlands: Eastwood Hall, Eastwood, Nottingham, Notts	07737 66111
London and South East: Coal House, Lyon Road, Harrow on the Hill, Middx	01 427 4333
South Wales and West of England: Cambrian Buildings,	
Mount Stuart Square, Cardiff, S. Glam	0222 21652
Northern Ireland: (Coal Advisory Service): 87 Eglantine Avenue, Belfast	0232 667924
Wood and Solid Fuel Association of Retailers and Manufacturers	
PO Box 35, Stoke-on-Trent, Staffs	0782 44311

BIBLIOGRAPHY

Ayres, James. *The Shell Book of the Home in Britain*. Faber and Faber, London 1981.

Barran, Fritz R. *Der Offene Kamin*. Julius Hoffman, Stuttgart 1976.
Bradbury, Kathleen. *Solid Fuel in the Home*. Women's Solid Fuel Council, London 1973.
Brown, H. J. C. (Ed). *The Fireplace Book*. Roshfield Publications Ltd, Windsor, Berks 1980.

Danz E and Menges A. *Modern Fireplaces*. Academy Editions, London 1979.
De Sterke, Freek. *Open Haarden*. Kluwer Technische Boeken BV, Antwerp 1977.

Edwards, Frederick. *Our Domestic Fireplaces*. Robert Hardwick 1865.
Elder A. J. *Guide to the Building Regulations 1976*. The Architectural Press, London 1977.

Fraser-Stephen, Elspet. *Solid Fuel Housecraft*. Crosby Lockwood and Son Ltd, London 1950.

Kelly, Alison. *The Book of English Fireplaces*. Country Life Books, London 1968.
Kern K. and Magers S. *Fireplaces*. Owner Builder Publications, California 1978.

Locke, H. B. (Ed). *Energy Users' Databook*. Graham and Trotman Ltd, London 1981.

Lytle, R. J. and M. J. *Book of Successful Fireplaces*. Structures Publishing Co, Michigan 1971.

Nissen, Helge. *Pejsebogen*. Nyt Nordisk Forlag, Arnold Busk, Copenhagen 1961.

Orton, Vrest. *The Forgotten Art of Building a Good Fireplace*. Yankee, New Hampshire 1974.

Pickering Putnam, J. *The Open Fireplace*. James R Osgood and Co, Boston 1882.

Seymons Lindsay, J. *Iron and Brass Implements of the English House*. Alec Tiranti, London 1970.
Shuffrey, L. A. *The English Fireplace and its Accessories*. Batsford, London 1912.
Sunset Books. *How to Plan and Build Fireplaces*. Lane Publishing Co, California 1977.

Tattersall, Robert. *Home Heating and Fireplaces*. Stanley Paul and Co Ltd, London 1977.
Thear, David. *The Woodburning Book*. Broadley Publishing Co, Saffron Walden, Essex 1978.
Thorpe, Simon J. *Chimneys and Fuel for Woodstoves*. Simon Thorpe, Dyfed, Wales 1980.

Vivian, John. *Wood Heat*. Rodale Press Inc, Pennsylvania 1976.

West, Trudy. *The Fireplace in the Home*. David and Charles, Newton Abbot 1976.
Wright, Lawrence. *Home Fires Burning*. Routledge and Kegan Paul, London 1964.

OTHER REFERENCES

Brick Development Association. *Brickwork – Domestic Fireplaces and Chimneys*. Brick Development Association, Winkfield, Windsor, Berks 1981.

Building Documentation (UK). *Commodity File 4 Chimneys*. National Building Commodity Centre Ltd, London 1979.

Dept of the Environment Advisory Leaflets. 30 — *Installing Solid Fuel Appliances*. HMSO 1977. 44 — *Curing smoking Chimneys*. HMSO 1972.

Lead Development Association. *Lead Sheet in Building*. Lead Development Association, London 1978.

National Building Agency. *Easiguide to Solid Fuel and Oil Heating in Housing*. Building Design Supplement, November 1979.

Solid Fuel Advisory Service. *Solid Fuel Heating*. SFAS, London 1979. *Approved Domestic Solid Fuel Appliances*: List No. 39. London 1982/83.

INDEX

Page numbers shown in *italic* type indicate illustrations.